PUTIN KITSCH IN AMERICA

Putin Kitsch in America

Alison Rowley

McGill-Queen's University Press

Montreal & Kingston | London | Chicago

ISBN 978-0-7735-5901-1 (cloth)
ISBN 978-0-2280-0038-9 (ePDF)
ISBN 978-0-2280-0039-6 (ePUB)

Legal deposit third quarter 2019
Bibliothèque nationale du Québec

Printed in Canada on acid-free paper

This book has been published with the help of a grant from the Canadian Federation for the Humanities and Social Sciences, through the Awards to Scholarly Publications Program, using funds provided by the Social Sciences and Humanities Research Council of Canada.

We acknowledge the support of the Canada Council for the Arts.
Nous remercions le Conseil des arts du Canada de son soutien.

Library and Archives Canada Cataloguing in Publication

Title: Putin kitsch in America / Alison Rowley.
Names: Rowley, Alison, 1971- author.
Description: Includes bibliographical references and index.
Identifiers: Canadiana (print) 20190125489 | Canadiana (ebook) 20190125497 | ISBN 9780773559011 (cloth) | ISBN 9780228000389 (ePDF) | ISBN 9780228000396 (ePUB)
Subjects: LCSH: Putin, Vladimir Vladimirovich, 1952- —Collectibles—United States. | LCSH: Putin, Vladimir Vladimirovich, 1952- —In mass media. | LCSH: Putin, Vladimir Vladimirovich, 1952- —Caricatures and cartoons. | LCSH: Putin, Vladimir Vladimirovich, 1952- —Influence. | LCSH: Political culture—United States. | LCSH: Kitsch—United States. | LCSH: Internet—Political aspects—United States.
Classification: LCC JK1726 .R69 2019 | DDC 306.20973—dc23

Contents

Acknowledgments

This book only exists because my friend Megan asked me to participate in a conference that she was organizing to commemorate the 100th anniversary of the October Revolution. The people at that event were the first to hear my ideas about Putin kitsch and their feedback was instrumental in moving the project along. Dinner conversations with Paul and Mark stand out in my memory, but an early morning chat with Annie proved to be even more important. Annie was the person who insisted that I "take the meeting" when I received an email from a publisher interested in my research. As I rode the shuttlebus from the hotel to the airport, I brainstormed about how to turn my conference paper (and companion article) into something bigger. By the time I got on the plane, I knew I was not only taking the meeting, I was writing this book.

A month or so later, I presented part of my research at another conference. I am grateful to the audience members who came to listen to the panel. Their questions and suggestions pushed my thinking in new directions, and it was especially important to see that my old friends Ron, Maria, and Karl did not think I was crazy for changing my research focus so suddenly and dramatically.

After that conference, I knew I wanted to work with my first editor Richard again. Richard is tremendously supportive, even when a project may be outside of his comfort zone, and he seems to have mastered the art of knowing when and how to push an author in order to make a book better. I am lucky to have him in my corner.

Over the next eight months, Putin kitsch took over my life and bled into all of my relationships. I was fortunate to find a number of students who were quite interested in kitsch too. Ryan, Matthew, and Liza sent me Putin memes when they came across them online. Aria insisted every day before class that she could not wait to read this book once it was published. Alexina and Althea listened to every idea and every doubt. Both of them gave me things that became illustrations in the text and the strength to keep writing when I was exhausted. My debt to them can never be repaid. Justin (and his mom) arranged to have a Putin garden gnome made and their gift made me squeal like a small child as I opened the package. My friend Donna has been giving me Putin calendars for years for my birthday, and she also made sure I knew about all kinds of Putin-related things on Twitter. I have loved sharing the Trump/Putin journey with her. I must also thank Alex, Alison, Ann, Camilia, Catherine, Daly, Denise, Dillon, Holden, Ilya, Jamie, Jess, Joanne, Kathy, Kristy, Mat, Mike, Nick, Sam, Simon, Suzanne, Tracy, and Yuri.

Closer to home, I am lucky to have supportive parents. It meant a great deal to me when my mother let me know that my father was in the habit of discussing my research with fellow resort guests and tourists whenever and wherever they travelled. His insistence that it was just fine to break down disciplinary norms in one's research pushed me (again) in new directions, and I hope he is pleased by this book. My mom's daily support for everything that I do as a scholar is different, but just as important, and I hope she knows that.

My husband David – who greeted the arrival of the Putin garden gnome with "You are not putting that on the nightstand, are you?" – accepted this project with grace, even if he did not always understand my obsession with Putin kitsch. If he was not so interested in US politics, it would have been much harder to complete this book and to justify how much money I have spent on sources. Thank you for having my back.

I dedicate this book to my sons. You two may never understand how much I love you (down to the cellular level), but you are the light in my life.

PUTIN KITSCH IN AMERICA

I.1   Putin finger puppet sold via ThisisWhatIThink store on Etsy.com.

Introduction

A New Talisman for
a New Millennium

Why would someone in New Hampshire make and sell the
finger puppet in figure I.1 of Russian president Vladimir Putin on
Etsy.com? Why is puppet Putin shirtless and holding a machine
gun? How are we supposed to see this item – child's toy, piece of
political satire, or object with sexualized connotations? These are
the kinds of questions that *Putin Kitsch in America* investigates.

As the book unfolds, readers will gain a clearer understanding
of how Vladimir Putin's image functions as a political talisman far
outside the borders of Russia. By looking at material objects – the
kitsch in my title – I will trace the satirical uses of Putin's persona, particularly how he serves as a foil for other world leaders.
What quickly becomes clear is that the internet is crucial to the
mass outpouring of Putin memorabilia that floods the world today.
That memorabilia, in turn, demonstrates a continued political
engagement by young people, even as some political scientists and
media pundits decry what they see as the opposite. After discussing
material objects, I will extend my analysis to fan fiction. Here, too,

the internet is at the heart of the story, since it is the most popular medium for distributing these works; indeed, without the internet, it would be hard to describe fan fiction as a mass phenomenon, which it surely is today. Drawing on more examples from material culture, as well as from slash (fan fiction that features sex between generally same-sex characters), this book further addresses the ways in which explicit sexual references about government officials are being used as everyday political commentary. The pornographication of mainstream American culture over the past few decades has already been noted by academics, and of course by politicians who evoke moral panics to score points and influence policy. Turning a critical eye to Putin kitsch shows how the number of such references skyrocketed during the 2016 US presidential election campaign, and suggests that the phenomenon is likely to still be important when Americans next return to the polls. Finally, the internet makes possible a totally new kind of kitsch – the virtual kind. An examination of how the Russian president's image circulates via memes and parodies, as well as through apps and games, suggests that political culture has become increasingly participatory in the last decade.

Despite the fact that pictures of Vladimir Putin's face (and naked chest) abound in the West, to date the scholarship on Putin's leadership cult has focused primarily on its media and material manifestations in his home country. A number of books and articles have outlined Putin's changing public persona and the kinds of media stunts that he has engaged in over the years. These works describe in great detail how Putin's masculinity is connected to the functioning of the Russian political system. Other experts have explored the kitsch that has emerged as part of the Putin cult in Russia. The wide array of products linked to Putin has also captured the attention of Western journalists, who regularly comment on the most extreme examples. This introductory chapter covers some of the same ground in order to explain how an obscure official came to occupy Russia's top job in 1999 (despite being on no one's political radar only a few months before), and how his celebrity status has been used to anchor him in power ever since.

It is impossible to understand Putin's meteoric rise in popularity without first grasping how hard life was for most Russians in the 1990s. While people in the rest of the world celebrated the collapse of communism and generally assumed that Russia would simply transition into a Western-style liberal democracy with a capitalist economy, they blithely forgot that similar transformations had taken hundreds of years in their own countries and had been accompanied by great hardship for millions of people.

Simply put, the 1990s were not a good time to live in Russia. The best year may have been 1997 when only 20.7 per cent of the population lived below the poverty line; that figure hovered slightly above or below 30 per cent for much of the decade.[1] Similarly alarming numbers can be cited for things like life expectancy, wage arrears, and capital flight. Russian women – with a life expectancy of seventy-two years – lived shorter lives than average Western women, but the drop-off for them was not quite as precipitous as it was for Russian men. By the turn of the new millennium, Russian men lived, on average, sixteen years less than their Western European counterparts; their life expectancy fell to only fifty-nine years.[2] Part of the problem may have stemmed from growing financial insecurity since wage arrears became a noticeable feature of everyday life from 1993. Within five years, the problem had grown to massive proportions with more than 66,000 firms admitting that they were an average of three months behind in paying their workers.[3] The Russian State Statistical Committee announced at the start of 1998 that the aggregate total for wage arrears was 50 trillion roubles (approximately US$8 billion).[4] Hyperinflation eroded the value of the wages that were paid. Money, to the tune of roughly US$20 billion per year in the mid-1990s, flowed steadily out of the country.[5] A full-on financial crisis hit in 1998 when Russia's currency, bond, and stock markets collapsed, leading to a 5.3 per cent contraction in Russian GDP and the need for an IMF bailout.[6] On top of all that, Boris Yeltsin's last year in office saw a series of terrorist bombings, contentious parliamentary elections, and a new round of fighting in Chechnya. When he finally resigned, Yeltsin's approval rating had sunk to just 4 per cent.[7] Is it any wonder that the Russian population longed for a bit of stability?

They found it in an unlikely place: Vladimir Vladimirovich Putin. Putin was born in Leningrad on 7 October 1952. His parents, though not an older brother Viktor, survived the Siege of Leningrad. The family's post-war lives were ordinary: they lived in a communal apartment with few amenities. Putin's mother worked in a factory and his father, who had been wounded fighting in the war, found a job as a security guard and later at a carriage works. In 1975, their son graduated with a law degree from Leningrad State University and went to work for the KGB. The first ten years of his career might best be described as plodding. Nothing indicated that Putin would rise to the highest echelons of power. He got married in 1983 and two years later was posted to Dresden in East Germany. There he watched the East German regime collapse, but from a distance. Dresden was not exactly at the centre of German political life. Two months after the Berlin Wall was dismantled, Putin returned to Leningrad. He took a position as an assistant to the vice rector at his alma mater, Leningrad State University, although most scholars assume that he also maintained some ties to the KGB. Putin's fortunes were deeply intertwined with those of Anatoly Sobchak, who became mayor of the renamed city of St Petersburg in June 1991. Sobchak assigned the task of heading St Petersburg's Committee for External Relations to his protégé, who may have used the opportunity to enrich himself and others.

The committee was supposed to import food for the city and pay for it with natural resources. Contracts amounting to $92 million were signed but the food never arrived. When a city counsellor tried to investigate, she found her efforts stymied and the event was quickly hushed up.[8] In July 1996 Sobchak lost his bid for re-election, leaving Putin adrift as well. In August, the latter moved to Moscow where he was named a deputy in the Kremlin property department.

Then suddenly, in July 1998, Vladimir Putin's career took off. In circumstances that remain quite murky, he was appointed to head the FSB (the successor to the KGB). A little over a year later, in August 1999, Putin stepped into mainstream politics when he replaced Sergei Stepashin as Russia's prime minister. At almost exactly the same time, a suspicious series of bombs exploded in Moscow, in Dagestan, and in the city of Volgodonsk. The next month Russian troops began a new military engagement in Chechnya. In other words, the country, which already seemed wracked by corruption and financial mismanagement, appeared to face new threats from "terrorists" and "extremists." In such a situation, Putin's police background was far from a handicap. Instead, Russians who were worried about the state of their country could choose to believe that Putin would deal with the crises firmly. From his very first public pronouncements, such as threatening to bump off Chechen terrorists in their outhouses, Putin began to cultivate his image as a strongman, what Russians refer to as a "silovik."[9] On the last day of 1999, Putin reached the apex of Russian politics: he became acting president when Boris Yeltsin resigned and appointed him his successor. Finally, on 26 March 2000, any lingering strangeness from that arrangement was seemingly laid to rest when Putin was elected president of Russia after only one round of voting.

From the moment he took the reins of power, Putin and his handlers (most notably Vladislav Surkov, who served as first deputy chief of the Russian Presidential Administration from 1999 to 2011) connected his public persona with very specific notions of masculinity. According to American journalist Steve LeVine, who covered Russian affairs for some of the world's most important newspapers for sixteen years, it was the "forty-three-year-old Surkov [who] was the mastermind behind the making of ... The Putin – the transformation of the president's visage into a savior-of-Russia icon, gargantuan and granite-faced, gazing from billboards, television screens, and newspapers throughout Moscow."[10] Putin's initial image did set him up as a saviour. His public persona revolved around traits such as sobriety, intelligence, and athleticism – all meant to distance him from Yeltsin, whose health and alcohol problems were an open secret at the end of the 1990s. Eliot Borenstein's research has demonstrated how in that decade Russian popular culture was preoccupied with fears of national collapse and the seeming powerlessness of Russian men in the wake of the Soviet state's disappearance.[11] Much of this cultural discourse was expressed in works that contained explicit sex, violence, or both. Under the circumstances, that made staid and stolid Vladimir Putin refreshingly boring (despite his occasional chest-thumping) – a beacon of stability.

The Russian public was introduced to its new leader via an enormous amount of politicized kitsch. Borrowed from German, *kitsch* is a strange-sounding word that suddenly emerged into relatively common usage in the second half of the nineteenth century. Merriam-Webster defines the noun this way: "something that appeals to popular or lowbrow taste and is often of poor quality."[12] The word almost always carries a derogative connotation and implies that an object, usually mass-produced, has a tackiness about it as well. Think Elvis collector plates and the Pope Francis calendar that I bought for my brother-in-law one Christmas at Walmart. Both are examples of kitsch. People who study it argue that kitsch's appeal is primarily emotional rather than aesthetic.[13] In the political realm, kitsch is, to quote professor of education Catherine Lugg, "a type of propaganda that incorporates familiar and easily understood art forms … to shape the direction of public policy."[14] And it consistently legitimizes the political status quo. In Russia, at the start of the new millennium, Putin-inspired kitsch was suddenly everywhere. For example, Susan Glasser, writing in an article for the *Wall Street Journal*, noted twenty-eight different Putin portraits available for sale when she visited a Moscow bookstore.[15] These portraits were intended to serve as office décor for low-ranking state bureaucrats. Her piece also mentions carpets, chocolate sculptures, and toothpicks with Putin's visage printed on them. Two chocolate portraits, each weighing more than 3 pounds and retailing for roughly US$700, were manufactured by the Russian firm Konfael in 2003, according to professor Helena Goscilo.[16] Goscilo's exhaustive research into the material expressions of Putin's leadership cult in Russia in the early 2000s also lists the following items emblazoned with the president's likeness: T-shirts, coins, pins, and an array of paper goods such as posters, postcards, and calendars like the ones in figure I.2. "His portraits in oil, Swarovski crystal, amber and semi-precious stones, copper, mosaics, and charcoal, as well as busts and full-figure sculptures," Goscilo notes, "became a booming business."[17]

Putin was certainly not the first Russian ruler to see his face splashed all over the media and imprinted on material objects this way. More than a century ago, the last emperor, Nicholas II, allowed photographs of his family to be published on picture postcards, and the 1913 celebrations in honour of the 300th anniversary of the Romanov dynasty led to a steady stream of royal souvenirs as well. Still, the tsarist government's efforts to drum up some positive propaganda appear tame when compared to the outpouring of material created by its Soviet successor. When the first Soviet leader, Vladimir Lenin, died in January 1924, the country was only just emerging from a prolonged civil war and a devastating famine. The new regime was far from firmly tethered to power,

1.2 Putin calendars for 2017 and 2018.

so Lenin's death had the potential to upset the situation entirely. For that reason, the Politburo members, who had been flirting with creating a leadership cult once it became clear that their comrade's health was fading in the early 1920s, launched a full-on media extravaganza when he finally died. Apart from an array of busts and monuments, over the next few years, Lenin memorabilia came in the form of jewelry, cigarette boxes, household wares such as teacups and plates, and even confectionary items.[18] Lenin was everywhere, and his image continued to fulfill a vital political role. Historian E.A. Rees explains the three functions of such a leadership cult this way: "Firstly, its role was to legitimise the power of the small ruling group around the leaders. Secondly, it was intended as a mechanism to manage and defuse the potentially explosive conflicts within the governing stratum itself. Thirdly, it aimed to manage relations between the ruling group, the governing stratum, and the wider society."[19] In other words, leadership cults are meant to ensure political and social stability.

The Soviet government never again went without one. The cult of Lenin gave way to the even more omnipresent cult of Stalin, although when the latter died, subsequent leaders toned down their efforts a bit. Still, with such a legacy, it is unsurprising that Kremlin officials fell back into the familiar pattern of celebrating a state official via media manipulation during the transition from Yeltsin's to Putin's leadership. They continue to do so despite the fact that Putin has now been in office for close to two decades and does not face any serious challengers for power.

With that said, at least two things make Putin's cult rather different from that of his predecessors. Yes, Kremlin officials carefully micromanage Putin's public appearances, so they can tweak his image to appeal to various constituencies, but they cannot unilaterally control all of the outcomes. Whereas in the 1920s, the Party's Central Executive Committee could simply issue two decrees that ensured total control over the use of Lenin's image, Putin's handlers have nowhere near that level of influence.[20] As we shall see throughout this book, the problem is the internet. Kitsch is always a product of its own particular moment in time and it changes as new technological possibilities open up. In their book on the history of computing in Russia, journalists Andrei Soldatov and Irina Borogan aptly point out that "the internet is the everyman's platform. To control it, Putin would have to control the minds of every single user, which simply isn't possible." Instead, they go on to say, "Information runs free like water or air on a network, not easily captured."[21] But it can be manipulated. Computers rework photographs and video clips easily, and reuse them irrespective of copyright. Once you mix together social media, print-on-demand services, and the explosion of fan fiction in cyberspace, you get a new kind of political landscape. This means that much Putin kitsch actually tells us something rather different from what one might expect: we learn what ordinary people think about the Russian leader, not just what the Kremlin wants us to believe. Moreover, the Putin-inspired materials erase what many people consider to be a hard and fast binary: the line between information and entertainment. As we shall see, much Putin kitsch amuses as it comments on politics.

The extreme sexualization of Vladimir Putin that was part of his mid-2000s image makeover also has no precedent. Lenin's clothing choices did not change once his party seized power; he dressed throughout his adult life in conservative, rather bourgeois-looking black suits. Despite the fact that he died when he was only fifty-three, party propagandists frequently portrayed Lenin as an ideal grandfatherly figure to children and described his relationship with his wife in comradely, rather than romantic, terms.[22] Lenin's extramarital affair with Inessa Armand was not revealed until after the collapse of the Soviet Union. To think of Lenin as a sex symbol was simply inconceivable and largely remains so to this day. For example, there is no Lenin underwear for sale on the internet; my Google search using those words autocorrected to "Linen under-wear" because it rendered no results. Similarly, typing in "Lenin thong" brought up the website for Thong Nhat Park in Hanoi – which Tripadvisor refers to as "a nice pleasant park with a statue of Lenin" – not any items of sexualized political kitsch.[23] Moreover, when the Russian Communist Party attempted to rebrand Lenin's image on its 2016 election posters, the move garnered contradic-tory reactions. In the most talked-about picture, Lenin appeared as a young man in his twenties, wearing jeans, sneakers, and a T-shirt, and carrying a laptop. He stood next to a very attractive young woman and Karl Marx, who had also received a makeover. According to the artist, the goal was to turn Lenin into a sex sym-bol, so the party would have more appeal to young voters.[24] The attempt failed. When the votes were counted, the party had fifty fewer seats in the Russian Parliament, and Putin's United Russia party scored an overwhelming electoral victory.

The contrast with Putin is striking. Since the mid-2000s Putin has been transformed into a man of action who, in carefully planned media events, has challenged wild animals, flown military aircraft, and even discovered historical artefacts while scuba-diving in the Black Sea. "Putin's stage performances," according to Russia experts Fiona Hill and Clifford Gaddy, "have the double advantage of not only ensuring his domestic popularity but also of keeping outside analysts confused about his true identity."[25] Historian Elizabeth Wood argues that the timing of at least some of those events is significant because they allowed Putin to be, as she puts it, "campaigning without campaigning," while he decided which job he would take as his second term as Russian president wound down.[26] Certainly, the world media watched closely and received quite a shock when the Kremlin website, Russian state television, and a number of Russian newspapers suddenly printed photographs of a half-naked Vladimir Putin in August 2007. Putin was on holiday in the Republic of Tuva in Siberia. The now famous photographs showed him fishing in the Yenisei River, as well as striding along the banks of the Khemchik River where he also paused to scoop up some water to drink. In each image, the president's bare chest is front and centre, marking him as a virile, physically fit, and ideally muscled man.[27] Given the rather remote setting, it is clear that the leader was touting his abilities as a frontiersman as well as his impressive physique.[28] The same can be said for the second and third sets of shirtless Putin photographs. Taken in 2009 and 2017, respectively, they reveal a relaxed leader enjoying the sunshine and some outdoor activities.

This new macho man of action was presented as wildly attractive to women.[29] Given that he was almost never photographed with his wife – the couple quietly divorced after thirty years of marriage in 2013 – Putin has been able to project the fantasy that he is an available romantic partner. In one 2012 poll, 20 per cent of Russian women stated that they would not mind marrying Putin.[30] Indeed, his sex appeal is fundamental to his grip on political power, as Putin's hyper-masculinity is now at the core of his public image as a ruler. It allows him to assert his dominance over not just the natural world and women, but his political rivals, who are always depicted in less masculinized terms by the Russian media.

Satirists have had a field day with these images of Putin on holiday, since they are so ripe for computer manipulation. The manipulations are so common that they have become quite banal. The last batch even sparked a "Putin Shirtless Challenge" on Instagram when Pavel Durov – the founder of the Russian social media site VKontakte who now lives abroad after clashing with the Russian government – called on his followers to start posting their topless photographs online.[31] In the past ten years, all of the shirtless Putin pictures have been doctored at one time or another. The resulting creations then circulate as internet memes or as images printed onto a seemingly endless number of material objects via print-on-demand services. Depicting the Russian leader without a shirt serves as a visual shorthand for the qualities that people ascribe to Putin's constructed persona, making him instantly recognizable – even if the quality of the facial features on some individual pieces of kitsch is so poor that they hardly resemble Putin at all.

Take this Russian postcard as an example (fig. I.3). Obviously, Putin has never literally ridden a bear, but that has not stopped this faked moment from becoming an iconic representation of the man. The choice of animal is not accidental. Instead, like many Putin objects, this image – which I suggest is a prime example of Putin kitsch – offers a number of interpretations depending on viewers' level of political engagement and knowledge.[32] Putin's United Russia party, for instance, uses a polar bear as its logo, so the postcard can suggest Putin's dominance over his direct political followers. A tinge of irony is added by the fact that Dmitry Medvedev, who replaced Putin as Russia's president from 2008 to 2012, has a last name derived from the Russian word for bear: *medved'*. Given that many people now view Medvedev as merely a

Нас не догонят

I.3   2016 Russian postcard.

temporary stand-in for Putin and someone who never had any real political independence, the postcard could serve as a visual pun, implying that Putin was always the alpha male in their partnership. In addition, Putin's pose evokes that of a medieval Russian warrior (*bogatyr*) on horseback, which is a familiar Russian trope given how many influential works of art, films, and political posters have used it in the past century and a half. A wider critical lens invites the interpretation that the bear, being expertly ridden and controlled, represents the country as a whole – a country that is again being forcefully directed by Vladimir Putin. Finally, a competitive element that no doubt appealed to Russian national pride is introduced by the caption on the postcard; "Nas ne dogonyat," can be translated as "You will not catch up to us." Without even needing another leader to appear in the frame or be referenced by name, the image suggests that Russia under Putin's leadership is doing better than other nations.

I have listed all of these readings because I want to show how even a relatively mundane and common bit of Putin kitsch is often much more complicated than a passing glance might indicate. It is items such as these that have firmly established Vladimir Vladimirovich Putin as an international celebrity.

———•———

What I have just written is important to Americans because, as I shall outline in chapter 1, they too use tropes of hyper-masculinity to assess their political leaders, whom they now also treat as pseudo-celebrities. In this context, Putin makes an ideal foil. Personality-driven politics and questions of character currently dominate the media landscape in the United States, thereby making scandals that expose the peccadillos of political figures a regular part of the news cycle. Changes in media – from the creation of twenty-four-hour TV news stations to the rise of the internet – only feed the frenzy. It is worth remembering that Putin is a notable figure on a world-wide stage, including in the American media. In 2007, *Time Magazine* named him "Person of the Year," while *Vanity Fair* dubbed him the world's most influential person in 2008. Even as protestors dismayed by Putin's possible return to the presidency filled Moscow streets in 2011, *Forbes* magazine was referring to the man as the world's second most powerful person. Love him or hate him, it is practically impossible to ignore Vladimir Putin, and he remains a lightning rod in the global public sphere.

Once we understand why Americans might be intrigued or enticed by the public persona of the Russian president, it is time to consider how material culture is being shaped as a result. Chapter 2 draws on examples from a number of different media to show how widespread the Putin kitsch phenomenon has become in the last decade. The form that kitsch takes is always distinctly tied to the era in which it is made. Consequently, the chapter describes in some detail how the rise of internet print-on-demand services has converged with current political discourse. These services let ordinary citizens upload designs that can be printed onto all kinds of paper and textile products; they make a political statement in the process. When politicized handicrafts, like the ones found on Etsy.com and discussed in this chapter, also enter the mix, we get a sense of how the production and consumption of Putin kitsch is a participatory process.[33] That is important because it contradicts the notion of an increasingly disengaged American electorate. Putin kitsch instead shows that at least some Americans remain passionately interested in politics, but they are using new methods to express their views.

The past decade has also witnessed a convergence between US politics and pornography. Pornographication, a term coined by communications scholar Brian McNair, refers to the bleeding of references and images from the world of adult entertainment into mainstream culture, particularly into areas where one would not expect them.[34] Its impact on politics stems from the fact that references to explicit sex can be used to satirize politicians and undermine their credibility with the electorate. That works particularly well in political systems – like the American one – that rely on constructs of hyper-masculinity to define their ideal leaders. As we shall see in chapter 3, an array of sexualized Putin kitsch – everything from buttons and stickers to colouring pages and T-shirts – was created during the 2016 US presidential election. The items played upon an imagined sexual relationship between candidate Donald Trump and Vladimir Putin. Putin's long-established, alpha-male image was manipulated by people wanting to suggest that Trump would be no match for the Russian leader. The more explicit materials attacked Trump by making him the passive partner in the duo's sexual couplings and by referencing all types of sexual fetishes. To a certain degree, these items found traction because of comments

Trump made on the election trail (indeed, one could even argue that he fostered their creation): never before had a candidate for America's highest office made public references to the size of his penis or to grabbing women by their genitalia. Given the scandals that plagued Trump's first two years in office – the Stormy Daniels story is still playing out, and the Mueller investigation into Russian interference in the election is ongoing as I write this book – this vein of Putin kitsch continues to be a rich one, meaning that the pornographication of US politics continues.

While chapter 4 introduces a new kind of kitsch – what I am calling fake fiction – to the discussion, we see some familiar tropes being expressed. Like most writers of fan fiction, the people who churn out fake fiction are not professionals, but they are keenly interested in their subject matter, in this case politics. Because fake fiction is self-published via Amazon.com, it offers an unvarnished glimpse into the imagination of its writers; there are no editors to tone down the prose, fix the grammar, or criticize a plot line. That leaves the authors free to do exactly as they please and jettison any kind of political correctness if they so desire. Their "what if" narratives build off actual political moments, such as election campaigns, summits between leaders, or scandals that threaten to disrupt international relations. In other words, just a veneer of truthfulness is included in the background details so as to suggest that the larger narrative could be real. However, fake fiction stories soon venture into more fantastic scenarios.

The earliest example that I have found unsurprisingly uses the image of Vladimir Putin in connection with Sarah Palin. I say unsurprisingly because fake fiction follows a similar trajectory to that of the material objects that are discussed in chapters 2 and 3. Palin's addition to the McCain ticket in the 2008 US presidential election coincided with Americans beginning to use print-on-demand services to express political opinions. The greater penetration of the internet into daily life made that possible, and it encouraged an increasing number of people to write fan and fake fiction as well. Palin's well-publicized remarks about Russia on the campaign trail were the butt of many jokes about her intelligence and fitness for office. We see that reflected in *Air Force Two: Going Rogue*, a fake fiction novel that depicts a world where McCain and Palin won the election. As in the real world, Putin serves as a foil for the American leaders who look far less competent than the Russian president.

Putin occupies the same position as a stereotypical evil mastermind in contests with former president Barack Obama. Obama's masculinity, and hence his fitness to hold America's top job, was constantly attacked during his time in office. Referencing tense foreign policy standoffs with his Russian counterpart was one way that fake fiction – like material culture – could suggest that Obama was failing. Putin only briefly stepped out of this role when people began to comment on the 2014 Russian invasion of Ukraine, an event that was viewed negatively in the West. At that point, fake fiction joined objects of material culture to shine a spotlight on Putin's own policies and actions. Russia's illegal and aggressive seizure of a neighbour's territory, for instance, sparked someone using the pseudonym Bacillus Bulgaricus to pen a story called *Putin Huylo and the Goldfish*.

Finally, a couple of fake fiction authors used imaginary sexual encounters between Vladimir Putin and Hillary Clinton to comment on the political ambitions of the latter. These works exemplify the pornographication of US popular and political culture – something that escalated quite dramatically during the 2008 election cycle and featured prominently when Americans went to the polls again in 2016. Relying on an unspoken binary, where any sexual fetish is seen as deviant, the writers use their extremely detailed descriptions of Clinton and Putin's escapades to, in essence, argue that neither is suitable for public office.

My discussion of sexually explicit fiction continues in chapter 5, where close to a dozen works of Trump/Putin slash fiction are analyzed. Slash narratives derive from homoerotic elements that fans observe in a relationship between two heterosexual men. Fans of television programs have been writing slash for fifty years or so. As growing internet usage has led to larger and more visible fandoms, the number of people posting slash works about their favourite book, movie, or television characters has simply exploded. Over time, slash writers have also used their keyboards to churn out "real people slash," in other words, stories about musicians, celebrities, and politicians. When the latter are the focus of attention, slash works often constitute a kind of political commentary that satirizes unpopular leaders and their policies. In this, they are reminiscent of the politicized pornography that has been around since the early modern era. The underlying premise of both genres is that certain monarchs or politicians are not appropriate rulers – a fact that is exposed when stories or drawings show these people engaged in acts that the mainstream would consider deviant.

Trump/Putin slash emerged within weeks of Donald Trump announcing that he was going to run for president, and works continue to appear, although admittedly with less frequency since Trump was inaugurated in January 2017. The same bromance that sparked the creation of so many pornographied material objects caught the attention of slashers, especially the ones who do not like the American leader. They created stories and novels – self-published on Amazon.com – that rely on familiar aspects of Putin's public persona to undermine Trump's credibility and masculinity. In almost all cases, Putin is presented as a superhero-like character whose naked pectoral muscles serve as his distinctive costume. Some narratives tap into Putin's love of animals and the outdoors to showcase his hyper-masculinity. Others assign supernatural qualities to parts of his body, notably the Russian's penis and the semen it produces. Finally, a third kind of Trump/Putin slash incorporates symbols of state and sacred political locations to suggest that Putin has a great deal of influence on contemporary American political life. In all of these instances, because the representations of the two men are set up in a binary fashion, the narratives imply that Trump is not man enough to govern the United States.

Finally, in the last chapter, I look at the ways in which Putin's image has been manipulated on the internet. Digital kitsch is emblematic of this moment in time, when Web 2.0 allows for greater and greater horizontal communication. While being mindful of the difficulties in knowing with absolute certainty what drives people to use digital technologies in this way, I hope to show the wide range of materials being created, as well as their playful nature. The long-running "Putin on the Ritz" meme, among others, shows exactly that. By now Putin's image is so ingrained in popular culture that references to it are easily understood by people across the globe, but it is more challenging to prove that they are using his likeness for overtly political reasons. Questions of civic engagement and popular culture are also at the forefront of my discussion of Putin-inspired smartphone apps and video games. Again, the evidence is both tantalizing and frustrating because, while many examples have been created, the motivations of developers and gamers remain largely elusive. Ironically, it is only when discussing Putin's presence – really his lack thereof – in the world of internet porn that I can feel quite confident in my conclusions. So much of this book has talked about the pornographication of American political culture that I expected to find many Putin mashups or parodies on xxx-rated websites. Instead, this ended up being the one part of the web where the Russian leader was missing. I think his absence underscores the fact that the other sexualized materials I have discussed were never meant to arouse anyone. Putin kitsch, then, remains purely a form of contemporary political discourse, but one that has the power to reach just about every person on our planet.

1

Scandal, Satire, and Masculinity in American Politics in the Digital Age

Conservative talk-radio superstar Rush Limbaugh was ranting as usual: "He can't take a punch, he's weak, and he whines … I'm sure some women find that attractive because they would look at him as a little boy and would want to protect him … But it embarrasses me as a man."[1] Limbaugh's target was Senator Barack Obama, who had just launched his run for the White House, and who, in Limbaugh's mind, was clearly unfit to occupy such a hallowed and powerful space. The words that spewed from his mouth might reflect contemporary American political discourse, but they are also a product of a media landscape that has changed dramatically in the past few decades.

A confluence of events made the 1980s a pivotal moment for news coverage in the United States. Scandals, like that involving Senator Gary Hart in 1988, led to a seemingly permanent convergence between tabloid journalism and news reporting. Advances in technology affected how quickly stories were reported and allowed journalists more freedom to roam. New television programs, and indeed entire channels devoted solely to news, made it difficult for ordinary Americans to avoid hearing about the indiscretions of their political leaders. The issue of "character," which had notably been raised in connection with Watergate, occupied a central position in political discourse, leading to a greater and greater personification of American politics in general. Politicians were increasingly treated as celebrities. These changes meant that news coverage of elections and policy-making initiatives came to be construed as personal competitions between designated individuals. Much of that competition was talked about in highly gendered terms, with pundits using what Meredith Conroy terms "gender conflict framing."[2] Their language – like that of Rush Limbaugh quoted above – ensured that masculinity was a crucial factor in determining who was elected and how effectively candidates could govern once they had been chosen by the public.

As these changes took root, displays of over-the-top masculinity on the part of politicians became routine. In fact, they were so routine that an entire genre of media satire emerged to mock them. Television programs like *The Daily Show*, as well as comedic websites such as JibJab.com, were created in the 1990s and continue to be influential. Their satire takes great delight in revealing the constructed reality of American politics and relies on postmodern irony for its punch. Viewers are expected to know a great deal about politics – fears about Americans' political disengagement notwithstanding – or they will not understand the humour. Satire, in this context, is an important corrective to a world grown increasingly facile. It serves "as democracy's feedback loop," in the words of Dr Russell Peterson, since it "can illuminate injustices, point out hypocrisy, and tell us when our government is not living up to its ideals, thereby raising the awareness that is the first step toward alleviating any of these problems."[3]

In the new millennium, more and more of that satire is found online. The internet has created a globalized public sphere where political commentary of all sorts is readily available. American politicians were initially slow to catch on to the power of this new technology. The year 2004 served as a kind of tipping point because the Howard Dean campaign benefitted from having a manager with a background in computing and marketing in addition to a love of politics. Dean was able to do incredible things in terms of fundraising and outreach via the internet, prompting other candidates to look closely at his campaign's methods. Subsequent election cycles have seen political figures embrace social media (with Facebook and Twitter accounts supplementing official websites) and data mining. However, greater connectivity has not enabled politicians to control what is said about them, or how their image might be manipulated. As we shall see, the very nature of the internet makes that impossible, thereby guaranteeing that scandal and satire continue to drive the news cycle distributed across the globalized public sphere.

Given the current parameters of American political discourse, it is not surprising to see constructs of masculinity and the personification of politics extended to foreign policy. During the deep Cold War, Soviet leaders were cast as the perfect foil for their American counterparts. Today that role is occupied by Vladimir Vladimirovich Putin.

———•———

In hindsight, it is easy to say that Gary Hart should have known better. In the middle of his campaign to secure the Democratic nomination in the 1988 presidential election, the former senator from Colorado got caught spending time with an attractive young woman who was not his wife. At first Hart was not worried about the allegations, because for decades there had been an unspoken rule in Washington: reporters did not write about any sordid episodes in the private lives of politicians unless they had some bearing on the political situation of the nation. Hart assumed everything would just blow over and the media would ignore what was going on in order to focus on policy issues. Instead, speculation about Hart's relationship with Donna Rice became a national soap opera that dominated the news cycle for weeks.

Both long- and short-term reasons explain why the Gary Hart scandal became a kind of ground zero in a new media environment. The Watergate scandal that brought down the Nixon presidency in the 1970s also cast the issue of "character" into regular American political discourse. It is important to note that in the previous decade, feminists had singled out marital fidelity as a more significant behavioural marker for men. Now, by the time Gary Hart was photographed with Donna Rice sitting on his knee, politicians increasingly faced questions about their moral fitness to lead, and those questions were asked by a generation of journalists taught to believe that their most important task was to uncover moments when politicians lied to the public. Journalists who had any qualms about reporting Gary Hart's sexual slip-up itself were mollified because, to quote from Matt Bai's first-rate study of the incident, "a story that proved he baldly lied about that same affair could be construed as serious journalism."[4]

By the 1980s, it was much harder to escape the glare of the media as well. New nightly television programs such as *Crossfire* needed news stories to fill up their allotted minutes. CNN, which debuted in 1980 as the world's first twenty-four-hour cable news network, required even more. The invention of videotapes, portable cameras that could record on them, and the first TV satellites allowed reporters to be more mobile. They could now literally chase after stories. In addition, these technological changes shrank the timeline needed for stories to catch fire, leading to a news cycle that began lurching from scandal to scandal. Television was vitally important here because of its apparent intimacy. As questions of character became central to how Americans evaluated their leaders, television – to quote communications scholar Hinda Mandell – "appeared to reveal a previously hidden 'essence' of the subject's nature and character."[5] The strong focus on candidates' personalities and values shifted political coverage ever closer to celebrity-driven tabloid reporting. The lines blurred even more once politicians started to add regular appearances on entertainment programs, particularly those hosted by late-night comedians, to their calendars. When Bill Clinton first went on *Arsenio* in 1992, it was a relatively novel idea. Twelve years later, during the primary season run-up to the 2004 US presidential election, all nine Democratic candidates appeared on one late-night program or another. By 2007, Republican senator John McCain actually announced that he was running for president on David Letterman's show. These spots garnered all sorts of attention due to a common kind of cross-pollination: the broadcast news picked up on the appearances and incorporated snippets of them into their own programming. They also gave candidates an opportunity to improve their likeability factor by showing "that he or she has a sense of humor, just like a regular person."[6] In the span of a decade and a half, television became the medium that could make or break a political figure.

There was no attempt to rein in the coverage either. Whereas in earlier decades the US government had imposed ethical standards on broadcasters, arguing that they provided a public service, such restrictions disappeared in the 1980s. The Federal Communications Commission (FCC) got rid of its "public trust" rules, which left broadcasters free to determine their own content and chase ratings. In his book *Tuned Out: Why Americans Under 40 Don't Follow the News*, professor David Mindich argues that the moment when "broadcasters began to conflate ratings and relevancy" was pivotal in the rise of sensationalist journalism.[7] In his words, "sensationalism's primordial soup needed three basic ingredients: (1) a media system that financially rewards people who reach large (or) larger audiences; (2) a level of competition that puts pressure on media companies and workers; and (3) a willingness on the part of one or more competitors to pander to prurient tastes."⁸ In simple terms, broadcasters and journalists discovered that crises of all kinds drew in wider audiences than detailed and thoughtful coverage of public or foreign policy, so a steady diet of scandal became the new normal and the basis for a great deal of news coverage.

This cycle of scandal has led to a greater and greater personification of American politics, as well as an erosion of faith in larger institutions. Campaigning and legislating are now regularly framed as personal competitions between rival politicians. In this world, it behooves candidates to position themselves as outsiders in order to distinguish themselves from others. That is why, to quote Joseph Cappella and Kathleen Jamieson, "Running against government, Washington, insider politics, and Congress is a stock-in-trade of federal elections."⁹ However, as Capella and Jamieson go on to say, the "result is an irony. Candidates are elected by undercutting the institutions of which they are or aspire to be a part."¹⁰ Moreover, the fierce tone used on the campaign trail does not disappear once elections are over. Instead, politicians regularly resort to personal attacks and competitive language as they pursue their legislative priorities. Compromise and collegiality fall by the wayside, making it more difficult for government to function effectively. In other words, the consequences of such rhetoric are serious. As members of the public become increasingly cynical about the gridlock they perceive to be afflicting the government, they look to ever more outlandish figures to fix (or upend) what they assume is a broken system. That, in turn, encourages media outlets to continue to focus on questions of personality and character. When flaws are inevitably discovered in elected officials, anything from a minor hiccup to a full-on scandal emerges, thereby feeding the twenty-four-hour news cycle for another day or week.

The emergence of twenty-four-hour cable news programming was not the only thing to change the way in which average

Americans consume political news. Just as MSNBC and Fox News went on the air to compete with CNN, new late-night programs, such as *The Daily Show* or its spinoff *The Colbert Report*, which debuted in July 1996 and October 2005 respectively, also turned their attention to the antics of politicians night after night – or, we could say, scandal after scandal. They differed from predecessors like *The Tonight Show* or *Late Night with David Letterman* in the amount of satire that they offered. Traditional late-night programs might have had a politicized opening monologue, but much of their contents fit the comfortable framework of a standard variety show. The "fake news" genre, on the other hand, was relentless in its critique of the world around it. Still, both streams of information have proven to be remarkably influential. In 2000, when the Pew Center polled Americans about what media sources they relied on to learn about presidential hopefuls Al Gore and George W. Bush, comedy and late-night variety shows beat out traditional sources such as Sunday morning talk shows, similar programs on cable networks, news magazines, and C-SPAN.[11] Nor was all the attention given to candidates running for the highest office in the United States; instead, all kinds of political figures found themselves to be the butt of jokes on television. Research by a trio of scholars showed that, between 1996 and 2001, the four main late-night programs contained a staggering number of jokes about politicians – 15,528 to be exact.[12]

These shows have been complemented by a number of internet sites devoted to political humour. *The Onion*, for instance, has been online since 1996 and millions have viewed its contents.[13] Likewise, JibJab.com was founded at the end of the 1990s. Known for producing funny animated Flash movies, the company has satirized political leaders since its inception. Early forays included "Ahhnold for Governor" (2003) and "This Land" (2004), which mocked George W. Bush and John Kerry as they faced off for president. The number of people who watched these productions is significant.

As word spread about "This Land," for example, the website was visited by up to a million people a day. Within three weeks of the film's release, it had been seen by 10.4 million people, or three times the number who had visited the official Kerry and Bush websites that month.[14] Similar parodies were created for every presidential election through 2016, and now their reach extends even further since the files are accessible on YouTube and can easily be shared via social media like Facebook.

The constant posturing and gamesmanship of contemporary political life only makes it easier for the satirists we have just been discussing to operate. Thirty years ago, in his book *Constructing the Political Spectacle*, Murray Edelman argued that the news had become a form of theatre, where political figures relied on the manipulation of language and carefully managed public appearances to craft a fake reality that kept them in power. The trick was convincing members of the public that this construct was real. That wound up being easier than one might think. "'The news' is made, reported, interpreted, and read by a small fraction of the population," Edelman wrote, "and it is ignored, resisted, or only intermittently noticed by the overwhelming majority."[15] In order to attract attention from the masses, news reporters and political leaders fed them a steady diet of stories constructed with alarmist language and simplified tropes. All that satirists such as Jon Stewart and Stephen Colbert had to do was create montages from material that already existed. And unlike traditional journalists, they did not need to watch what they said for fear of losing their access to information.[16]

Concerns about the impact of all this satire – particularly the question of whether it causes people to disengage and grow cynical about politics – have been voiced for the past decade. Scholars and pundits, with the exception of those who study what has been termed "participatory" or "DIY" culture, regularly wring their hands when they are asked about the subject.[17] Whether one agrees with their assessments or not, it is true that the popularity of programs like *The Daily Show* and *The Colbert Report* can be connected to the rise of postmodern irony. Lisa Colletta's excellent work on this subject, which I will talk about in more detail in the next chapter, describes postmodern irony as one that is above all self-referential. It also obliterates distinctions between what is real and what is fake. Instead, it assumes that all reality is constructed. In this world, as Colletta notes, "Politicians perform their roles with a smirk and wink aimed at a television audience, knowing that saying something is true is equivalent of its being true, that appearing is the same as being."[18] It falls to satirists to bring the absurdity of those moments into the open, which they do on a nightly basis on American television.

In the debate over whether postmodern irony is a positive force for change, or a negative force that could lead to the destruction of democracy as we know it, I fall on the positive end of the spectrum. I agree with Dannagal Goldwaite Young and Sarah Ersalew, who have argued that *The Daily Show*'s humour actually says that "something better is possible."[19] The kinds of sources that I work with, and that fill the pages of this book, say the same thing. They show a deep level of political engagement, even if it is not expressed in traditional terms. Here, satire functions as an important social corrective that shocks people into recognizing their own assumptions and forces them to think about alternatives.

It should be noted that some of that satire I have been talking about deliberately references explicit sex to make its point. That should not be surprising. At a number of key junctures in human history, when political establishments were wobbly, everyday people turned to pornography to express their opinions. In the decades leading up to the French Revolution, for instance, pornographic pamphlets attacked the country's social elites. They referenced the bodies of political figures as a means of desacralization. By presenting aristocrats as impotent or the king as a cuckold, they called the legitimacy of the ancient regime into question. "If the king could not control his wife or even be sure he was the father of his children, including the heir to the throne," writes historian Lynn Hunt, "then what was his claim on his subjects' obedience or the future of the dynasty's claim to the throne itself?"[20] Similar questions were raised about the last Russian emperor Nicholas II, who was swept from his throne in February 1917. As rumours spread about Rasputin's relationship with the empress, the monarchy lost much of its divine lustre and remaining political support. Pornographic cartoons and verses suggested that the Siberian faith-healer was the real father of the heir to the throne, while hand-drawn postcards showed the empress's naked breasts being fondled by Rasputin. These materials relied on laughter and mockery to undermine the power of the tsar.[21] But they had a much smaller reach than the kinds of pornographied political kitsch we see today. What fuels the current flood of sexualized political satire is the internet – a technology that no national government can fully regulate or control.

Sex scandal-driven news cycles did not disappear in the years since Gary Hart's political career was ruined. Instead, we now live in a world where no one thinks it strange that Wikipedia has entries for "List of Federal Political Sex Scandals in the United States" and "List of State and Local Political Sex Scandals in the United States" – because, frankly, there have been so many scandals that it is hard to keep track of them all. Mandell's research drew on 134 incidents, with the median year of her sample being 2007. She argues that that was a particularly important year, technologically speaking: the iPhone was unveiled, and new Blackberry models were also released. Both devices had newly developed chat features and cameras, attracting people to such technology and changing how they used it. That same year Twitter was launched, and the number of Facebook users surged to 50 million from only 5.5 million two years earlier.[22] Over the next decade the numbers continued their upwards trend, until Facebook revealed in mid-2016 that it had 1.65 billion active monthly users.[23] These figures demonstrate the emergence of something that media expert Brian McNair terms the "globalized public sphere" – in other words, a "digitised, networked information space."[24] This is the space where much political discourse now takes place.

Despite the rather meteoric rise in internet usage, politicians were slow to embrace or even understand what was happening. They did not realize that a growing number of young people were spending more time on the internet than watching television, and that the shift was about to make old-style campaigning less effective. A few tentative early forays into cyberspace stand out; the first came in 2000 when Senator John McCain ran against Bush for the Republican presidential nomination and his team raised more than $6 million in online donations.[25] Others came in 2004, the year that Facebook was founded. For instance, MoveOn.org – a progressive public policy advocacy group that formed in response to the Clinton impeachment scandal in 1998 – ran a contest encouraging ordinary people to use digital technologies to make anti-Bush commercials.[26] The site then posted the work of fifteen finalists online for the world to see. Democrat John Kerry was the target of a smaller, but still important, digital attack the same year. In his case, someone photoshopped a picture to make it look like Kerry had attended a 1970 rally against the Vietnam War with Jane Fonda (a figure whom many conservative voters find repugnant). The picture then went viral.[27]

But their efforts were completely eclipsed by the fundraising that the Howard Dean presidential campaign was able to do online; it received the kind of money and attention that suddenly vaulted its candidate to the front of the pack. Bottom-up politics was the name of the game for the Dean campaign, and the decentralized nature of the internet fit it perfectly. Of course, Dean benefitted from having Joe Trippi serve as his national campaign manager. Trippi, who combines a passion for politics with a background in computing, was perhaps the first person to truly grasp how the internet was changing politics. His book about the campaign describes many instances where handlers had to explain to the candidate why all this internet stuff was important, but as the money poured in and campaign events grew larger and larger, Dean came around. The campaign website – and its blog – became a nexus for communicating with supporters. Whenever staffers posted a flyer for an event on the site, they received a flurry of emails with suggestions or improved versions. Sometimes people went even further and sent in computer code that improved the software the campaign was using to publicize and organize events. Finally, the contents of the Dean blog spurred supporters to use their own blogs to discuss the candidate's policy positions; Trippi argues that these "politically savvy, objective bloggers serv[ed] as de facto campaign reporters."[28] What Trippi emphasizes throughout his book, and what will be a central argument in *Putin Kitsch in America*, is the participatory nature of politicized online communication. "In fact, it was the opening salvo in a revolution," Trippi writes; "the sound of hundreds of thousands of Americans turning off their televisions and embracing the only form of technology that has allowed them to be involved again, to gain control of a process that alienated them decades ago."[29]

Since those words appeared, American political campaigns have become far more tech savvy, but so too have the people who respond to them, who form the basis of the globalized public sphere. Print-on-demand services began to connect political commentary with material goods in the 2008 US election cycle (more on that subject in the next chapter). Simultaneously, the Obama campaigns became particularly well-publicized role models for data management and how to connect with individual voters across the United States. Yet, the very nature of the internet meant that states and other hierarchical institutions were correspondingly losing their ability to control political narratives. As professor of digital media and global affairs Taylor Owen puts it: "Large media organizations have held power over the global information environment through three levers of control: access to information, access to infrastructure, and the creation of journalistic norms. In each of the areas, digital technology is challenging the control held by the intersection of state and corporate interests that have long shaped the media narrative."[30] Owen argues that the kind of collaborative networks one finds online allow people to share power horizontally and to become emboldened in the process, since they are protected by a certain degree of anonymity. He connects various movements – from the Arab Spring to Occupy Wall Street to the actions of Anonymous – to what he sees as a new form of social organization, one that is ad hoc but passionately committed. The groups Owen studies "rely on technology to facilitate open communication, avoid hierarchy in their organization and planning, and embrace direct political action against an old world, perceived (rightly or wrongly) as ineffective, corrupt, and statist."[31] The reason I like his words so much – enough to quote them at length – is that they also apply to the political processes I see at work in the production of Vladimir Putin kitsch. It, too, is a kind of direct attack on the perceived political status quo in America, and it cannot be controlled by any party or organization.

But why Vladimir Putin? The answer is quite simple. First Soviet and now Russian leaders have been a – some might even say *the* – yardstick against which American political leaders are measured. During the Cold War, candidates for office were routinely evaluated on the basis of how aggressively they would handle Russian-American relations, and government leaders justified large amounts of military spending because of the perceived threat from the other side. As early as the late 1940s, and continuing through the 1950s, conservative Republicans turned to tropes of masculinity and sexuality to undermine their political enemies. They labelled many long-standing foreign policy officials as "effete homosexual Communist sympathizers subverting America from within."[32] The Democrats too eventually attacked their Republican counterparts for being "soft on communism," although it must be said that their charges lack the elements of homophobia found in earlier Republican rhetoric. John F. Kennedy, for instance, repeatedly blamed Dwight Eisenhower and Richard Nixon for the spread of communism into Cuba, and he insisted that the previous Republican administrations had allowed America to fall behind in the missile race with the USSR.[33]

In these decades, foreign policy was often quite literally reduced to a contest between two men whose bodies served as proxies for their nations' respective political and economic systems.[34] Again the Kennedy presidency provides an example of what I am talking about. Kennedy suffered from all kinds of health problems – most notably a bad back that sometimes made movement difficult for him – but that did not stop his administration from cultivating an image of their young leader as a vigorous and athletic kind of guy. Muscular masculinity was a central tenet of Kennedy's political reputation and his rhetoric, particularly when he took on Soviet leader Nikita Khrushchev in the early 1960s.

For their part, the Russians played along during this Cold War contest, and they continue to do so. That is because their leaders, especially Vladimir Putin, also have a masculinized, militarized ethos at the heart of their political culture. The situation allows American political commentators to feel very comfortable deploying familiar media frames when they speak about Russian leaders. For instance, while in no way supporting the actual Russian invasion of Crimea in March 2014, Fox News personalities were impressed by how Putin handled himself at the time. Report after report spoke about Putin's decisiveness and leadership, while also noting the tepid response from US president Barack Obama. The incident was framed as a gendered fight between the two men, although it is unclear how Obama could have acted differently short of also invading part of the Ukraine. But logic does not always matter in these instances. Instead, viewers were bombarded with emotionally charged (and grammatically challenged) comments like this one from Sean Hannity: "So we got a community organizer against a former KGB leader who is getting his butt kicked and embarrassed and humiliated on the world stage … the picture of Putin swimming the butterfly, which is a real hard stroke. Yeah, big chested – and by the way, it's in frigid water that he's swimming across a river … so you got a picture of that juxtaposed next to Obama on a bicycle in Martha's Vineyard with the goofy helmet on riding his bike."[35]

This one comment says much about why and how the Russian president has become so central to American politics. In an age when celebrity and spectacle routinely trump substance, Putin is the perfect foil for anyone who wants to comment about political leaders, particularly in a negative way. As we shall see in the next chapters, Putin kitsch – much of it the product of the digital age – offers people new avenues to do just that.

2

We Are Living in a Material World and Vladimir Putin Is a Material Boy

In 2016, 14 million colouring books for adults were sold in the United States, making them one of the most important segments of the book market.[1] Such things are not new; colouring books for adults have actually been around since the 1960s, but the current boom in sales has brought them to a new generation.[2] When scholars and journalists discuss the trend, the same idea – that colouring books of flowers and geometric patterns are therapeutic and help relieve stress – is presented over and over. Politicized examples that do not fit with that rather placid image are typically left out of the discussion. However, Amazon.com has many such colouring books listed for sale, and they need to be considered, since such works reflect how important internet commerce has become to the ways in which people use material culture to express their political views.

"Welcome to this Color Therapy book, by Colorful Coloring Books. Each page is filled with a unique piece of art for you to enjoy coloring," wrote the maker of the *World Leaders Coloring*

Book. But they did not stop there. The rest of the statement on the opening page packs quite a punch:

> Have you had a hard day at work? Feel like shit? Want everyone to Fuck Off? If that is the case, this Color Therapy book is ideal for you! Do you hate politics and just want every political leader to leave the planet? This Color Therapy book will allow you to take out your political frustrations by coloring in 25 of the world's most influential leaders. We hope you enjoy yourself coloring and feel the burdens of stress ebb away!

In this instance, as well as in other examples such as the *Manly Color: Coloring Books for Men Book 10 Political Edition* and the *This Guy Sucks Ass Adult Coloring Book*, Vladimir Putin is just one in a gaggle of political leaders to laugh at. In a later offering, however, he does not have to share the limelight. The *Vladimir Putin Adult Coloring Book* was published by Diane Kirkwood via CreateSpace on 30 November 2017. As befits Putin's larger-than-life image, on the title page Kirkwood describes her work as a "New Tsar and Russian President, Strongest Political Leader in the East and Oligarch Inspired Adult Coloring Book."[3] Colouring in these contexts offers a carnivalesque subversive thrill, since it is possible to express one's dislike for a politician by making them appear as ridiculous as possible.

The appeal of the colouring books, particularly for those who make them, is also financial. When *Business Insider* profiled Jenean Morrison in December 2015, it revealed that the Memphis, Tennessee, resident had sold more than 90,000 copies of her self-published colouring books, and made nearly half a million dollars in the process.[4] Morrison, who specializes in floral patterns, sells her work via CreateSpace, the self-publishing platform that Amazon acquired in 2005. She is just one of many people who have discovered that self-publishing can be quite lucrative. Over the past half-decade, the number of self-published book titles has grown by 218.33 per cent, according to Bowker, the official ISBN agency for the United States. That means that in 2016, 786,935 ISBNs were assigned to self-published works.[5] Now with only a few clicks of a mouse, the CreateSpace platform can turn someone's uploaded PDF into a paperback book, which is then listed for sale on Amazon. The books are print-on-demand, so authors do not need to have any kind of manufacturing facility or production deal. Nor do they concern themselves with distribution since Amazon handles that too. In exchange, authors receive about a 40 per cent royalty of the list price for every book sold. Importantly, authors also retain total creative and editorial control of their work, meaning that in the case of politicized colouring books, there is no one who can, or will, censor their political message – making this kind of political kitsch beyond the control of any government or public institution.

And, I might add, Amazon is not the only game in town. Ben Thomas of Omaha, Nebraska used a Kickstarter campaign to partially fund *Adventure Buddies Youuuge Book of the Coloring for Winners*, a Trump-Putin themed colouring book created by his publishing start-up company, Bumblebot.[6] There are also individual Vladimir Putin colouring pages available for sale on Etsy.com. Buyers who purchase these receive a digital file to download, print, and then colour at their leisure. Finally, if someone does not wish to pay for the privilege of, say, giving Putin green hair and bright red lipstick, it is possible to find free colouring pages on the web as well.[7]

More importantly, as the pages that follow show, colouring books are just the tip of the Putin kitsch iceberg. By deliberately drawing on an array of kitsch, and items that span a decade, we can see how Putin's image, particularly the muscular torso that seems to define him as a strong male leader, has become an increasingly important talisman – a lightning rod if you will – in US politics.

Changing technologies, sometimes in the manufacturing processes that allow for the easy production of kitsch and sometimes
in the ways that items are brought to market, are central to the
story. They remind us that political kitsch is always a product of
the capabilities of its era. In the past decade, internet print-on-
demand services have done two things: drastically increased the
number and kinds of items that can be politicized, and reduced
the control that politicians, and the image-makers behind them,
have over their own likenesses. Nor are these services the only
places one can look for Putin kitsch. As the final part of this
chapter demonstrates, the internet has also created a global market for handicrafts that address political subjects. These items are
important because they counter alarmist claims made by some
pundits who fear that successive generations of Americans have
grown increasingly disengaged from politics. Instead, the material goods show that the nature of political engagement is simply
changing and that making kitschy objects is an increasingly popular way to express one's opinions.

———•———

Americans have been living with Putin kitsch for more than a decade.
It is a prevalent and largely unquestioned part of the Western political landscape, even if the man's constant media stunts now garner
a steady stream of eye-rolls as well as new kitsch. But this was not
always the case. Putin did not seem all that special when he first
took over from Boris Yeltsin. Many experts in Russian-American
relations were caught off guard since they had never heard of
Vladimir Putin before he became Russia's leader. And if the experts
did not see this move coming, you can be sure that the American
public did not anticipate it. As I mentioned in the introduction,
Putin was picked to replace Yeltsin in part because his deliberately
boring and conservative image was a welcome change from the

unpredictability of his predecessor, whose time at the helm is not remembered fondly by Russians. To put it mildly, Putin in his first years in office was about as far from becoming an American celebrity as you can get.

Putin kitsch only burst onto the scene in the United States, in a sustained way, after the Kremlin website posted pictures of the bare-chested Russian president fishing while on holiday in the Republic of Tuva in August 2007. The timing is interesting. Putin was well into his second term as president at that point, and with sky-high approval ratings, there was no real reason to revamp his image, at home or abroad.[8] Except now he could. Putin could jettison his staid look in favour of something more dynamic and action-packed because Russia was entering a new phase in its relations with the West. The signals were there as early as January 2005, when Russia repaid its debt to the IMF three-and-a-half years early. Then in the summer of 2006, the Russian government paid off the last of its foreign creditors, meaning that the country was no longer beholden to anyone.[9] This allowed Putin to adopt a more aggressive foreign policy, and, not surprisingly, his public persona underwent quite a revision.

The 2007 images caught everyone's attention; political leaders were not known for taking their clothes off and showing their pectoral muscles to the world. Photos of shirtless politicians existed, of course, but they tended to be private family snaps that no one thought to turn into political propaganda. Nor were such images splashed across every form of visual media imaginable. Only occasionally did someone deviate from that established norm. It happened in fascist Italy, for instance, when Benito Mussolini staged several photo-ops to show off his muscled torso. In those action shots, he helped farmers bring in the grain harvest, flew a plane, and went skiing. "As a propaganda tool," writes historian Alessandra Antola, "the photograph of the shirtless Duce ticked all the boxes, conveying virility and athleticism whilst demonstrating the accessibility of the ruler, who came across as spontaneous even though the photograph was completely staged."[10] But when unauthorized photographs taken just prior to his first inauguration showed a shirtless Barack Obama on holiday with his family in Hawaii, it proved to be a controversial moment.[11] Some people were outraged at the seeming invasion of his privacy and the presumed assault on his dignity. No one has ever been outraged on Putin's behalf, however. That is because Putin, like Mussolini, authorized this change to his brand. It was part of the makeover that transformed the ordinary leader into an action-hero celebrity-style president.

The Putin photographs might have been forgotten in a few weeks if Americans had not already begun to embrace the print-on-demand services available on the internet. Such services were first connected to politics during Ron Paul's run for president in the 2008 US election. Without the candidate ever endorsing their actions, some Ron Paul supporters started to use CafePress to churn out kitsch for their man. They made all the usual things one sees in an election cycle – bumper stickers, T-shirts, buttons – but they did not limit themselves to reproducing the official "Ron Paul Revolution" logo. CafePress let them be far more creative with their designs. Soon the site was awash in Ron Paul memorabilia, and the candidate was being taken much more seriously by the mainstream media as his polling numbers spiked with all of the new attention. No one had ever seen anything like it before. Yet as one campaign volunteer remembered: "The official Ron Paul Campaign had nothing to do with any of it and all this activity went on below the radar of the mainstream media."[12]

What is CafePress, and how did it so profoundly affect the nature of American politics, even if no one really noticed that right away? CafePress was founded in San Mateo, California, in 1999 by Fred Durham and Maheesh Jain. The company has since gone public, and even after Amazon entered the print-on-demand market (more on that in a few pages), it remains an important player. By February 2006 – shortly before Ron Paul voters started using it – CafePress already offered more than 200 million possible combinations of products available for sale.[13] Via its website, the company lets users upload all kinds of images and text which can then be printed on a host of products. Its online storefront then sells the products to anyone who wants them. The items are strictly print-on-demand, so designers never have to concern themselves with logistics.

And this is where we find our first print-on-demand Putin kitsch. While unfortunately no print-on-demand services make their sales figures available to the public, CafePress does keep some of its designs for a really long time, and the listings tell you the dates when images were initially uploaded. (Other sites that offer similar services, like Zazzle.com, have no dates – truly maddening when you want to use them for research purposes.) That is how I know a designer who chose to remain nameless uploaded the image in figure 2.1 to CafePress on 10 August 2008. Almost ten years later, it was still possible to have this printed onto the baby bib seen here. Loudly proclaiming Putin to be a "real man," the picture – one of those taken during his 2007 Tuva vacation – fits with the Russian leader's newly created image as an alpha male who seems to go without some of his clothes on a regular basis. Indeed, unless one was a particular connoisseur of shirtless images of Putin, it would be easy to confuse this photograph with the ones released to mark later presidential vacations.

By fall 2008 references to Vladimir Putin were also creeping into the US presidential election. That year John McCain chose the governor of Alaska, Sarah Palin, as his running mate. Once she joined the ticket, Palin's gaffes became the butt of endless jokes in the media. In an 11 September 2008 interview with ABC News's Charles Gibson, Palin replied to a question about whether Alaska's proximity to Russia might give her any insights by saying: "They're our next-door neighbours. And you can actually see Russia from land here in Alaska."[14] History does not

2.1 "Vladimir is real man" printed on a baby bib.

remember that phrasing, however. Instead, people quote comedian Tina Fey's line from a *Saturday Night Live* skit mocking
Palin, and now the sentence "I can see Russia from my house" –
words that Palin never actually said – has become one of her
most iconic statements. Misquotations like this one are rife in

history and they continue to resonate with the public because they reveal, in the words of professor Ryan Milner, "a discursive truth beyond specific facts."[15] In our case, a designer named "Alessandra" invented a kind of imagined dialogue between Palin and Putin on this very subject. Two weeks after the original ABC News interview aired, and of course after Fey had skewered the vice-presidential candidate, Alessandra uploaded a design to CafePress (fig. 2.2). Featuring a picture of Putin wearing a fur hat, the text said: "Comrade Sarah, I can see Alaska from my house." The ominous tone of his fake reply reminded people that the political neophyte would be up against a far more experienced and nefarious foe should she be elected. It also suggested that Putin, like an evil mastermind, was closely watching events in the United States.

The irony is that by then Putin had withdrawn from much of the day-to-day running of Russian foreign policy. In December 2007, Putin, who was coming to the end of his second term as president, announced that Dmitry Medvedev was the man he hoped would replace him, and that he intended to take the job of prime minister. This manoeuvre was a blatant attempt to get around the term limits spelled out in the Russian constitution, but it meant that Medvedev became the public face of the Russian regime after he was duly elected in March 2008. For the next four years, people speculated about his relationship with Putin and the extent to which Medvedev was able to wield political power independently from his prime minister. Many world leaders, however, acted as if Medvedev was in charge and, according to Fiona Hill and Clifford Gaddy, the "assumption was that if Putin needed or wanted to know something, Medvedev would let him know."[16] Putin, in turn, avoided meeting with, or even taking telephone calls from, foreign heads of state.

It should not be surprising that the vein of Putin/Palin kitsch dried up when the McCain-Palin ticket lost in 2008. Barack Obama won,

2.2 Button from 2008 US presidential election that uses Putin to mock Sarah Palin.

and for the next eight years he served as a political foil for Putin, even as the latter devoted more of his attention to domestic issues, at least until he reclaimed the Russian presidency in 2012. When the pair were depicted together on material goods in the US, tests of physical strength often loomed large. Given the media focus on both men's bodies that is hardly shocking. The competitive angle, however, is part of a larger trend – one where politics is talked about using the language of sports and military conflict. Janis Edwards, a communications professor and expert on political cartoons, argues that "sports, heroism, and other metaphors used in reference to presidential candidates organize around the unique features of the dominant, hegemonic ideology of masculinity which … equates power with physical force and achievement."[17] That is a fancy way of saying that sports metaphors make some politicians look manly and capable, and make others appear less up to the task of governing or handling foreign policy crises.

Dan Youra, a conservative political cartoonist who lives in Port Hadlock, Washington, maintains an extensive array of his work on his website utoons.com. He also uploads some of his cartoons to Zazzle.com, a lesser known print-on-demand website, where they can be emblazoned on all kinds of products.[18] I used Zazzle to buy a postcard of "Superpowers," a cartoon Youra drew in 2013 in response to what he saw as Barack Obama's failures in Syria.[19] In the image Youra pits the two presidents as Atlas-like figures symbolically carrying the weight of the world on their respective shoulders. Whereas Putin's bulging muscles seem to have no trouble with his globe, Barack Obama lies squashed beneath his, instantly conveying the idea that he is no match for his Russian counterpart, that he is the lesser man.

Putin's physical domination of his rival is also implied in a design posted to Zazzle (fig. 2.3) by someone who uses the pseudonym "Putinator," whose seller profile picture is a photograph of Putin as a cyborg, and whose online store is named "PutinTheInInPutin." In other words, it is not much of a stretch to assume that our designer is a Putin fan. The joke hinges on a double entendre for the word "spanked." Obviously, the picture shows adult Putin disciplining a child-like Obama in short pants, as if the latter has been naughty. Since both men are fully clothed, the image should not be read as a sexualized one – like the ones we will see in the next chapter that speak to the Putin/Trump relationship. Instead, a different dynamic is at work. One of the criticisms of Barack Obama when he first ran for president was that he lacked experience; the point was made frequently in political cartoons in 2008.[20] Pundits suggested that he would be no match for his political rivals, including Vladimir Putin. In contemporary American speech, since "spanked" can also mean to utterly defeat your rival, the meaning is obvious: Putin wins again.[21]

2.3   Putin spanks Obama.

And the stakes got even higher after the Obama presidency ended. As the 2016 election campaign geared up, the amount of Putin kitsch circulating in America – particularly in the form of cheap textile products – exploded. All it took was a celebrity candidate who seemed to rather like the tough guy in the Kremlin.

———•———

A century ago, T-shirts were only worn as underwear and by men. Today, they are an integral part of people's wardrobes irrespective of age, gender, and wherever they happen to be in the world. The messages that T-shirts can convey allow people to present themselves without saying a word. To quote fashion journalist Charlotte Brunel, "In a word, the T-shirt is to clothing what the blank sheet of paper is to writing — a surface for imagination and free expression to run wild."[22]

The wearing of T-shirts originated in the United States navy just prior to the start of the First World War. During the Depression, when money was tight for so many, civilian men also began to wear the new shirts because they were cheap.[23] T-shirts received another boost in the Pacific theatre during the Second World War, since the weather there was often far too hot for standard military uniforms. At this point, it became acceptable to sport T-shirts as outerwear, and the presence of American servicemen in Europe also made the shirts fashionable there as well, particularly among young people. Within a decade, T-shirts were being widely made across the European continent.

T-shirts were first connected to American politics in 1948 when some were made — bearing the slogan "Dew it with Dewey" — for US presidential candidate Thomas E. Dewey.[24] Dewey might have lost the election to Harry Truman, but his new form of election kitsch caught on. During the next election, Dwight Eisenhower's campaign also opted to have T-shirts made, and soon their production became a staple in the American political landscape. It also became easier to turn what had been simple white shirts into walking billboards when a new kind of ink was invented in 1959. Plastisol was a durable and stretchable ink that made sure printed designs did not wear off or become distorted in a short amount of time. In the 1960s, the development of silkscreen inks further improved the quality of images on T-shirts. Now seen as unisex garments, T-shirts advertised products, proclaimed school affiliations, and publicized people's favourite music.

T-shirts, of course, have continued to be common features in the political arena for the past half-century since they are cheap to produce — certainly they cost significantly less than television or radio advertising. Computer software can now easily print transfers of almost any image (sometimes after it has first been manipulated); to make a T-shirt then simply requires that someone apply the transfer to fabric using a heat source. The process is so simple that it allows for a kind of "cottage production" where enterprising small manufacturers issue a steady stream of T-shirts that reference current political events. As Alice Harris points out, "In an election year the T-shirt in the United States is as visible as the American flag. A pollster's dream source for studying ongoing trends, it champions candidates, even while disembowelling their faux pas and foibles."[25]

Putin is an international symbol whose likeness has been printed on countless T-shirts and whose image pervades popular culture across the globe. That is only possible owing to the changing technologies that I have just described. Mass production is central to the widespread dissemination of Putin's image on textile products. However, it is important to note that print-on-demand services make it possible for the same image to appear on all kinds of things, meaning that there is not always a connection between the message and the form of the object it appears on. When the same design can be used on everything from baby bibs to throw rugs, it is hard to argue that the form adds to the political message of the overall item. With that said, there is one exception. When someone prints sexualized images of Putin on articles of clothing that fit closely to sexualized parts of the body, that obviously augments the impact of the items. The underwear that is discussed in the next chapter is a good case in point. But so too is the Putin bathing suit that can be seen here in figure 2.4.[26] Part of what makes the suit amusing is the placement of Putin's eyes over the breasts of the person who is presumably wearing it, and the possible ways in which that person's body could stretch and alter the Russian leader's overall appearance.

Obviously, Putin did not sanction the use of his face on swimwear. I doubt very much that Beloved Shirts, who made our bathing suit, asked for permission before they posted the design on their website, and in this they are no different from the other bigger

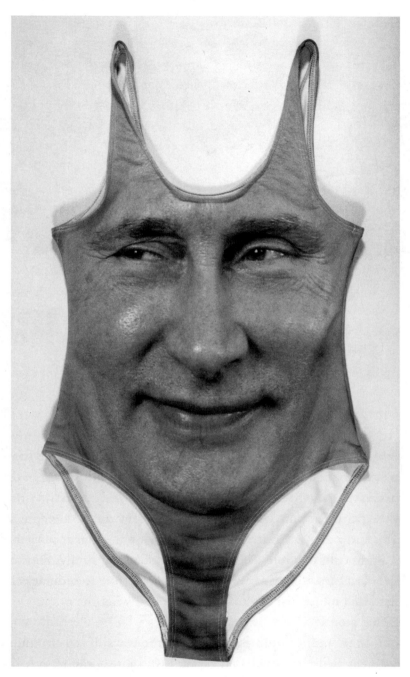

2.4   Putin on a bathing suit.

2.5 "Let's Make History Together" T-shirt.

print-on-demand services.[27] The technologies used by these firms are evidence of a loss of control on the part of political elites. In the Russian case, the Kremlin simply cannot control all facets of Putin's public persona in an age when computers rework photographs so easily and reuse them irrespective of copyright. That means that the Putin cult, to quote scholars Julie Cassiday and Emily Johnson, "accords a surprisingly active and even playful role to ordinary citizens: each individual determines for himself what the presidential brand denotes."[28]

To show that playfulness, as well as the ways in which Putin's image has infiltrated media far beyond Russian shores, let us consider the two T-shirts that are reproduced in figures 2.5 and 2.6.

Both images remain entirely consistent with the strongman persona that Putin presently cultivates at home, yet they are products bought in an American market. The first, figure 2.5, takes a famous photograph from the February 1945 Yalta Conference, crops it to exclude British prime minister Winston Churchill, and then superimposes the faces of Donald Trump and Vladimir Putin over those of US president Franklin Roosevelt and Soviet leader Joseph Stalin. The shirt was first listed for sale on Amazon.com on 1 September 2015 and is a product of Market Monkeys, an online retailer based in the Philippines. The image can be interpreted in several ways, although given the details that I have just offered about the manufacturer, I may be overthinking things. Some manufacturers are not overly motivated by politics at all, but by profit. Amazon's 2015 launch of "Merch by Amazon" – a T-shirt print-on-demand and order fulfilment service – opened the floodgates when it came to T-shirts for sale on the internet. At first, anyone could use the service, which did not require minimum orders. As is the case for colouring books, Amazon handles all of the logistics: it prints the submitted designs, ships the T-shirts, and deals with customer service queries. Unlike eBay, which charges sellers a listing fee and takes a percentage of the sale price, Amazon only keeps $9.80 from each T-shirt sold (the general list price is between $19.95 and $30), meaning that that participants in the "Merch" program have fewer upfront costs and do not need to store their own inventory.[29] The service proved to be so successful that Amazon has had to tweak its business model and restrict the number of vendors. Now people interested in working with "Merch" must apply to do so, and acceptance is not guaranteed. Despite the restrictions, this T-shirt market is extremely lucrative and requires even less infrastructure for small sellers than the printing of transfers described earlier.[30]

To return to the T-shirt in figure 2.5, certainly to scholars and no doubt some purchasers the doctored photograph comments on the perceived friendship between Trump and Putin by referencing another surprisingly warm relationship – that between Stalin and Roosevelt. But it also casts Putin as Stalin's surrogate. That fits with some Russian efforts to rewrite the Soviet past for the benefit of the current leader. In the words of Helena Goscilo, "The Kremlin's determination to control the portrayal of history, its withdrawal of various archives declassified during the 1990s, and its promotion of a study guide for high school teachers that characterizes Stalin as 'one of the most successful leaders of the USSR' rightly or wrongly strengthen the perceived parallel between the two authoritarian rulers."[31] It is doubtful that most Americans know of the specific actions mentioned by Goscilo, but that fact does not reduce the power of Putin's overall celebrity status. To the average American, Putin, whether they like him or not, is recognizable as a strong leader in the Stalin mold.

Our second T-shirt – figure 2.6 – taps into the notion that Putin is an arch political mastermind by suggesting that he is the power behind the scenes of Donald Trump's presidential campaign. Given the accusations of Russian meddling in the politics of a number of adjacent countries, as well as in the elections of several states in Europe, the underlying message of the T-shirt is not so far-fetched. Moreover, the T-shirt was made long before the Mueller investigation into Russian interference in the 2016 US election began: it was available as early as 1 September 2015 on Amazon.com. The manufacturers, "Think Before You Vote Campaign Shirts," took advantage of the listing's product description box to offer some political commentary. Prospective buyers were told: "We have an opportunity to shape the future of America in this election. Vladimir Putin does not need more influence in this country." They were also encouraged to vote for Hillary Clinton since "Her [sic] and the Democratic Party are the best hope for the future of America."

Other T-shirts, some of which will be talked about later in the book, reveal the extent to which Putin's credentials as an alpha male are so strong that his image then becomes an ideal instrument

2.6 "Think Who Are You Really Voting For?" T-shirt.

for satirizing other political leaders, most notably Donald Trump. That dynamic was evident throughout the latter's entire election campaign and remained strong in the first year of the Trump presidency. I briefly stopped buying Trump/Putin kitsch after the

November 2016 election results were in, but even though more than two years have passed, a cursory glance at the Amazon, eBay, or Etsy websites shows that new T-shirts keep popping up. Some of them look forward to the 2020 election, while others continue to imply that Trump and Putin have a sexual relationship (more on that later). To find them requires little skill. Merely typing "Putin T-shirt" into the search boxes on the home pages brings up page after page of listings. For example, on 16 August 2017, when I typed "Trump Putin T-shirt" into the search box on eBay.com, I got almost 1,500 listings. Moreover, I restricted my analysis to only those search parameters. A recent article by Jane Caputi, which analyzes the content of Trump and Clinton memorabilia from the last election cycle, also had a wealth of objects to draw upon. Caputi references all kinds of T-shirts, bumper stickers, buttons, and caps that were created via print-on-demand services and then worn by partisans of both candidates.[32] As her work, and mine, shows, it has never been so easy to market, profit from, and purchase political kitsch.

———•———

Part of the reason Putin kitsch is so fascinating stems from its participatory nature. Nowhere is that more evident than when we consider the handicrafts that are for sale on Etsy. Created as an online artisanal marketplace in 2005, Etsy had close to 450,000 registered sellers – whose annual sales were $26 million – within two years.[33] After altering its terms of service to allow for the sale of manufactured, as opposed to strictly handmade, items in 2013, the company experienced even more rapid growth, although its reputation as a hub for small businesses remains intact. In 2014, Etsy's gross merchandise sales reached $1.93 billion and the company went public the following year.[34] The company's valuation was set at $1.8 billion and it raised $237 million during its IPO. By November 2015, Etsy had 22.6 million active buyers purchasing items from its 1.5 million sellers.[35] Those sellers list items either through their computers or via a specially designed mobile app. They pay Etsy $0.20 per listing as well as a fee amounting to 3.5 per cent of the price when an item sells. Listings remain on the website for four months, assuming the products do not sell before that time elapses.

Etsy has some truly great kitsch. I am still kicking myself for not purchasing the Vladimir Putin garden gnome that was put up for sale in a store called Kretacean in November 2017.[36] The statue features a shirtless Putin emerging from the turret of a tank; the tank's gun resembles an erect penis pointing at the viewer. Even the product description is delightfully playful and clever, since it is plum full of Putin references, showing that the maker of the statue is well aware of Putin's recent actions. "He's coming to invade your neighbours' gardens," writes Sniglart, the owner of Kretacean, "and he might even decide to turn up to the G8 summit in his armoured car ... yes, by popular request, and with no fear of poisoned umbrellas, I present ... Vladimir Putin, the garden gnome." If purchasers dare to place the hand-painted acrylic polymer statue in their gardens, Sniglart, with tongue in cheek, warns that they "risk him herding ... other gnomes into a gulag!!!!" The store sells a whole host of politically incorrect gnomes of other world leaders. Only the one of the Russian president is overtly sexualized, but that is not terribly surprising given how deeply the image of a shirtless Putin pervades contemporary popular culture.

While I am sure that hand-painting a gnome takes several hours, once it has left Sniglart's hands, the resulting item does not ask much of its new owner. You open the package, remove the gnome from the wrapping, and put it outside in your garden where you can torment your neighbours who take their gardening (and perhaps their politics) more seriously. Other items on Etsy, notably the Putin-themed cross-stitch patterns, demand a much deeper level of participation from purchasers. Two patterns – both by StitchBucket – are noteworthy, although they are not the first ones on the market. The honour of developing the first pattern goes to a Russian woman who sent her pattern in to the newspaper *Komsomol'skaia pravda*; the design reproduced a photograph of Putin wearing sunglasses and a rain hat, but of course no shirt.[37] Cross-stitch patterns are just that: patterns. They are most definitely not finished products. Instead, purchasers receive a downloadable PDF file with instructions, including a list of threads to buy, complete with the required codes to get the right shades and a detailed sewing guide. Both designs from Etsy show Putin without a shirt. That is not particularly jarring in the first instance (fig. 2.7), because the Russian leader, who is often depicted as a sex symbol in the media, is on his own, and the suggestive caption makes his partial nudity seem like it is part of a seduction rather than simply weird.

On the other hand, Putin's naked chest jumps out much more in the second image, standing as he is beside a fully dressed Donald Trump (fig. 2.8). Although the owner of the store labels this image "BFFs," those letters do not appear in the design. The romanticized relationship between the pair is only conveyed by their clasped hands and the three small hearts that float above their heads.

It is a significant time commitment to complete these projects, since cross-stitch is done by hand. So, as someone pulls thread after thread through the fabric, what goes through their minds? If they initially bought the pattern because they found the picture amusing or subversive, is that reaction amplified as they look at it over and over? Do they hang the finished item on the wall, or give it as a gift to someone with similar political views?

One of my students, Althea, decided that she wanted to make these Putin patterns as a form of stress relief during a busy semester. She rather gleefully emailed me after she completed the first line of one of the patterns. When she received word that inclement weather had cancelled her classes one Tuesday in

2.7   Cross-stitch of shirtless Vladimir Putin.

2.8   Cross-stitch: "BFFS."

January 2018, Althea was pleased to get some extra time to work on Putin. "It is crazy to watch him take shape with every row," she told me in an email. A few weeks later, when she reported that a bit over half of his body was now complete, Althea tacked the following comment onto her message: "He was an absolute hit with my family this weekend; I think everyone is invested in his development." Moreover, excitement concerning the second project was already building. "My grandmother," Althea informed me, "is particularly excited to see how Trump shapes up on the next one." Her grandmother also started a phone call a few days later with "Does he [Putin] have pants yet?" In other words, the Putin cross-stitch was still on her mind days after she initially learnt what Althea was up to.

What I took away from these conversations was the degree to which the cross-stitch became an interactive experience. While Althea sewed it, a much wider circle of people – including fellow students, her relatives, and our departmental administrators – became invested in its progress. The project was a topic of conversation and laughter for weeks. Once it was finished, many people took photographs of it, thereby extending its potential impact even further; those pictures can be looked at multiple times and shown to even more people. Althea also decided to make a couple more – one to keep and one to give as a gift to a friend studying Russian history. Recently, Althea also gifted a finished Trump/Putin cross-stitch to a guest speaker who visited our department to discuss her research into political handicrafts.

The questions of motivation and engagement are sometimes possible to discern by focusing on Etsy sellers rather than on purchasers. I bought some fantastic hand-drawn Putin greeting cards from AryanaBraun in fall 2017 (fig. 2.9). The woman who makes them is named Jessica and she lives in Seattle, Washington. The little picture of her that appears on the order confirmation page shows her wearing a pussy hat – an actual bright pink, hand-knitted hat just

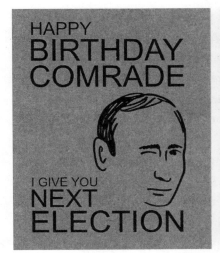

2.9 Hand-drawn Putin greeting cards.

like hundreds of thousands of women wore when they marched to protest the election of Donald Trump. As a result, I think we can safely assume that Jessica's cards meld her political views with a desire to make a bit of money. When she mocks Russian interference in the American election, as she clearly does with the caption of the birthday card I show here – or by playing with the notion of Putin's desirability to women, which she does in the other card – Jessica conveys something of her political worldview. What we have here is an example in which Putin kitsch can be subversive, and it offers a kind of safe space for people to express their displeasure with the political status quo.

That is important because for the past decade or so many political scientists, communications professors, and media pundits have been concerned about the influence of satire – particularly as it is expressed via television programs such as *The Daily Show* or *The Colbert Report* – on the actual political engagement of everyday Americans.[38] In a thoughtful article published in the *Journal of Popular Culture*, Lisa Colletta addresses that question head on.

She argues that the popularity of programs reflects the rise of post-modern irony, in other words, irony that is self-referential and full of cynical knowingness. Politicians in such a world are performers who seemingly value appearances more than substance; they are always on the lookout for their next photo-op and soundbite. Their words then create a discourse that is as unreal as anything that appears on television. Comedy shows have emerged, in turn, to reveal the hollowness of contemporary politics, its practitioners, and the news networks that provide such facile coverage of events. The danger lies in the effects of all this satire. As Colletta puts it, "does the smirky, self-referential irony that makes all of these shows so popular actually undermine social and political engagement, creating a disengaged viewer who prefers outside irreverence to thoughtful satiric critique and ironic, passive democracy to discerning, engaged politics"?[39]

Putin kitsch is no doubt full of postmodern irony, but it also shows a deep and sustained engagement with the political realm. Colletta concludes that for political satire to be deemed truly effective, it must lead to people actually turning off their television sets.[40] Maybe. Or perhaps she is looking in the wrong places to see the kinds of engagement that political satire is producing? I think that is why the Putin-inspired colouring books, handicrafts, and politicized textiles, to say nothing of the fan fiction that will be discussed in later chapters, are so important. They show people actively and creatively responding to the world of "fake news." They are part of what a much smaller number of academics refer to as "participatory" or "DIY" culture. My husband has on more than one occasion shaken his head as I've held up another piece of Putin kitsch to show him, or when I've talked about my research for this book; he always says, "I don't get it." I usually counter with, "You are not supposed to get it. My students get it." What I mean is that we are the wrong generation. My generation (and the ones that are even older) supplies just about every media commentator that you see on American television, and you would be hard-pressed to find many university professors with tenure who are below the age of forty. We grew up before the internet revolution and, to generalize, we are slightly less wedded to our gadgets and technology than people who were born after the internet became part of everyday life. That means that we typically think of political engagement in terms of more traditional behaviours like volunteering to canvass door to door for candidates, attending a political rally, or formally joining political parties. The behaviour that I have described in this chapter – where people respond to political events by creating and sometimes selling kitsch via the internet – does not fit into that older narrative.[41] It is something new and it is changing the nature of politics. Just how far the discourse influenced by objects of material culture has shifted will be even more apparent in the next chapter where we talk about the use of explicit sexuality to score political points.

3

Hardcore Kitsch

*Vladimir Putin, Donald Trump,
and the Pornographication of the
2016 US Presidential Election*

It was never my intention to start this chapter by referring to
another colouring book. But then *Putin F*cks Trump: An Adult
Coloring Book for Patriots* popped up on the Amazon sites in a host
of developed countries in early April 2018, and the symmetry was
simply too good to pass up. Whereas in the last chapter, I used politicized adult colouring books, among other things, to discuss the
role of internet commerce in the production of Putin kitsch and to
argue that the items that emerge in this new marketplace demonstrate a continued and deep engagement with political events, here
the focus is on sex. Sometimes the items that we will consider are
merely suggestive; in other instances, a detailed knowledge of pornography and various fetishes is needed to understand the subtext
of the images printed onto material objects. Sex in this context is
not meant to arouse. Instead, the explicit images are weaponized
the same way that pornographic images were harnessed in order to
make political statements during the French and Russian revolutions. However, by focusing on material culture, this chapter goes

further than earlier studies of politicized pornography, which could only look at pamphlets, drawings, cartoons, and graffiti.[1] Since the production of kitsch is so strongly connected to the technologies of its era, the past ten years or so have opened up new possibilities, allowing pornographically inspired political commentary to bleed over into an array of material goods that are not usually sexualized. That convergence is what I mean by the term pornographication, a concept this chapter will explore via the relationship – real and imaginary – between Vladimir Putin and Donald Trump.

As a colouring book, *Putin F*cks Trump* technically pornographies a genre that most people still associate with children, even though the adult market has been strong in the past few years. Every one of its twenty-five pictures is explicit – twenty-three show US president Donald Trump being sodomized by his Russian counterpart, while the remaining two feature scenes with oral sex. Sometimes props such as dildos or a tube of lubricant appear alongside the rutting men. In other cases, the pair are depicted in a variety of BDSM gear, including harnesses, restraints, and masks. In one instance, Trump has a ball gag emblazoned with a hammer and sickle logo stuffed in his mouth, and the book's front cover imagines the two men having sex on the desk of the Oval Office, one of the most sacred spaces in American politics. In the end, nothing about this colouring book is appropriate for children, but it is not an isolated example.

Indeed, since Donald Trump announced his candidacy in the 2016 US presidential election, there has been a steady deluge of materials like this. They demonstrate, in the words of American cultural critic and essayist Laura Kipnis, that "pornography can provide a home for those narratives exiled from sanctioned speech and mainstream political discourse, making pornography, in essence, an oppositional political form."[2] The sources considered here are quite specific in who they attack. The people who make the items assume an audience that is familiar with the public image of Vladimir Putin. By putting an imagined, same-sex relationship at the heart of their political satire, and by assigning Putin the dominant position in that partnership, the makers of our kitsch express their dislike for Trump and mock the traditional hyper-masculine constructions that define the American presidency.

———·———

As Shakespeare once wrote, "All the world's a stage." And it is certainly a more interesting one when you are playing with Vladimir Putin finger puppets and fridge magnets. While some people might consider these items part of what journalists have termed the "Peter Pan market"[3] – in other words, products designed for young people who refuse to grow up – others will see them as another form of interactive kitsch that allows people to laugh at current leaders and express their political opinions. The form makes sense in that case because it is possible to characterize contemporary politics as a kind of theatre, where, in the words of media studies professor Geoffrey Baym, "Governance is seen as drama and spectacle, while politicians are said to be role-playing on the public."[4] Still, the line is not always clear; sometimes even the manufacturers themselves do not seem sure how to characterize their own products.

That is definitely the case with the WWF World Finger Fight set sold by YTKid on eBay (fig. 3.1). The box says the toy is for children ages three to six, and the fact that the set comes ready to assemble, meaning the paper puppets can be made without needing tape, glue, or scissors, would indicate that children are indeed the target audience. (Frankly, adults in their forties whose finger dexterity is declining also appreciate these features.) But why on earth would small children want finger puppets of Vladimir Putin, Donald Trump, Kim Jong Un, Xi Jinping, and Rodrigo Duterte? I doubt kindergarten-age kids would fully

3.1 World Finger Fight finger puppet set.

grasp the world domination scenarios suggested by the stages provided with the set, either. The kit includes a general map of the world, as well as ones of Asia and the United States, to use when the leaders face off against one another. Finally, the minutiae used for puppet Putin only make sense if you are a politically engaged adult. As usual, Putin is the only person depicted without a shirt, but this time a small hammer and sickle has been painted on his chest. His communist-era past is not the only thing referenced by the toy makers, however, because Putin is also given a speech box that says "Send them to see God."

In other words, the text alludes to his tough-guy image, while at the same time referring to the fact that Putin has overseen a renewal of the Orthodox Church in Russia. It is quite a complicated message for such a small toy to give.

Children under the age of three are not supposed to play with the Bad Hombres Magnetic Play Set either (fig. 3.2). Made by the Unemployed Philosophers Guild, the set can be bought on eBay. It lets people dress Putin and his American counterpart however they want in a variety of clothes and props. The set relies on reduction – a basic technique of political cartoonists – to make its point. As professor of journalism Chris Lamb puts it, "Satirists try to reduce their victims by removing them of their rank, status, and clothes, showing the world that there is nothing underneath all the beautiful roves except an ordinary mortal."[5] As one can see from the cover image, in this instance, a thorough understanding of the events of the 2016 US presidential election campaign is also required for all of the accessories to make sense.

And yet eBay categorizes both of our items as toys. You can tell from the suggestions for more purchases that are given during the check-out process. For instance, I was offered three different Pokemon products when I bought the World Finger Fight set, and a vintage Playskool Humpty Dumpty puzzle and Melissa and Doug Farm Sound Puzzle with the Bad Hombres magnets. The algorithms that spit out these suggestions are clearly missing the political overtones of the sets. Part of that confusion must stem from the fact that puppets – and I am counting dress-up magnets as a kind of puppet here – are polyvalent symbols. They are childhood toys that can be fixed with some very adult meanings.

Putin puppet-inspired images and products appeared all over the internet in the fall of 2016. On 19 October, Hillary Clinton and Donald Trump squared off for their third and final presidential debate. At one point, Clinton referred to Trump as a puppet of Vladimir Putin. Trump answered her charge by insisting, "You're

3.2 Bad Hombres magnet set.

3.3   Donald Trump as Putin's
puppet colouring page.

the puppet." The term has frequently been used about the wives of politicians, since they are often depicted as mere mouthpieces for their husbands. This view, according to communications professors Karrin Anderson and Kristina Sheeler, implies "that there is a proper role for women in relation to men. They are invisible, follow behind, and are available to be used and manipulated for whatever

3.4   Campaign button that casts Putin as a puppet master.

cause."[6] Certainly that would be the impression conveyed by the colouring page created by Jenny, owner of the ColoringTrumpLand store on Etsy (fig. 3.3). Here, Putin is the man pulling all the strings during Donald Trump's circus-like political career. Irrespective of what Clinton actually meant by her comment, this was it – the trigger for a new wave of Putin kitsch, particularly concerning his perceived relationship with Donald Trump. Within days, buttons like figure 3.4 were available for sale.

Soon the kitsch took on a sexualized tone as well. It is worth remembering that puppets can also be seen as a type of sex doll whose body can be manipulated for the pleasure of the puppeteer. Indeed, a Trump blow-up sex doll could be bought on the

3.5 Thong with image showing
Trump as Putin's puppet.

internet during the presidential election campaign; the doll came
with a permanently erect penis and its box was decorated with
fake endorsements from Hitler and the KKK, among others.[7] The
focus on Trump's penis was, for its part, sparked by the candidate's
own comments during a nationally televised Republican primary
debate. Anyone wanting to see the footage can find it on YouTube.[8]

After Marco Rubio made a derogatory comment about the size of Trump's hands, Trump immediately fired back: "[The implication is] if they're small, something else must be small. I guarantee there's no problem. I guarantee you." Since that was the first time a potential American president had ever discussed the size of his genitals on television, it was a moment that stood out in public consciousness. Those words made it possible for all pictures that showed Trump as Putin's puppet to have a sexualized meaning, since it was now actually possible to imagine the candidate as a sex doll. The images on the button shown earlier, as well as on the thong in figure 3.5, can then be read as implying that Trump serves as a sex toy for Vladimir Putin, the dominant figure in their partnership.

The sex toy analogy bled even further: onto a T-shirt that reworked the logo of a popular American children's television cartoon. The program, *CatDog*, follows the misadventures of conjoined siblings, one a cat and the other a dog.[9] Created for Nickelodeon, the cartoon first aired in 1998 and ran for four seasons. In total sixty-eight episodes were made, and re-runs continued to be shown on Nicktoons through 2011. After that, episodes of *CatDog* were bundled with a number of other 1990s programs and ran on TeenNick until March 2013. The longevity of the show means that its logo is an instantly recognizable symbol for many people under the age of fifty. (I am including both the people who watched *CatDog* as children and their parents, who, like me, had to endure many hours of it while their kids monopolized the TV.) In the retooled logo featured on the T-shirt, the conjoined siblings become Trump and Putin – "Trumputin" instead of CatDog (fig. 3.6). The faces of the two men are also superimposed over those of the main characters. In a typically postmodern ironic fashion, then, the logo inspires a different meaning for those in the know. "Trumputin" looks like a sex toy – a double-headed dildo to be exact.

Why is it important that children's toys and the artwork from their television programs were becoming politicized and

3.6 T-shirt with logo that reworks the logo for *CatDog*.

sexualized? The simple answer is that it reveals what some people see as the pornographication of American society. The convergence of mainstream culture and pornography has been on the minds of scholars for the past two decades. In 1996, Brian McNair published a book called *Mediated Sex: Pornography and Postmodern Culture*. In it, he coined the term "pornographication" and described some of the ways in which porn was slipping into the mainstream. While other academics sometimes take issue with his definitions and conclusions, there is no denying the impact that McNair's work has had. Two more books – *Striptease Culture: Sex, Media and the Democratisation of Desire* and *Porno? Chic! How Pornography Changed the World and Made It a Better Place* – have updated McNair's original findings. In them, he shows how the process of pornographication is an ongoing and evolving one because it is tied to the emergence of new technologies, such as VCRs and the internet, which make the consumption of porn much easier. As McNair puts it, "the capacity to produce content and have it accessed by global publics represents an enhancement of popular power, an erosion of the traditional elite hold on the means of intellectual and cultural production."[10] As people consume more porn, they find it easier to spot and grasp references to it when these appear in more mainstream places. In other words, pornographic subtexts (like the one found on the *CatDog*-inspired T-shirt) become another kind of postmodern irony, and can be used to provide satirical comments about a whole host of subjects.

How does pornographication work? The most concise definition can be found in a journal article by Karrin Anderson.[11] To summarize: first, images, narratives, and references jump from the world of pornography into the mainstream. Next, hypersexual or exploitative elements are present even if an image or product may not actually be a piece of pornography. Finally, sexuality is introduced into arenas that are not normally sexualized, and, using humour or parody, individuals who defy traditional gender norms are schooled. Right away it should be apparent that much of the Putin kitsch that I have already discussed fits into this framework, and we have not even touched upon some of the most blatantly pornographied items yet.

They are not hard to find. CafePress, the online retailer of user-customized products that was founded in 1999, makes lots and lots of Putin products, including underwear for both men and women, such as the thong shown in figure 3.7.

I think the double entendre of the caption speaks for itself, and fits well with Putin's image as a sex symbol. Another thong listed on its website just has a picture of Putin, but lets the purchaser add any caption or name that they want to the finished product, thereby allowing people to be as bawdy or personal as they desire. It is the

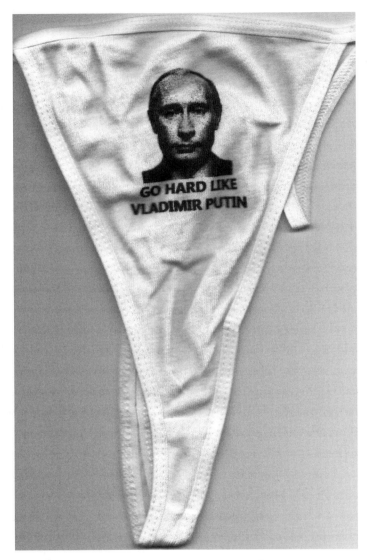

3.7 "Go Hard Like Vladimir Putin" thong.

perfect example of participatory kitsch. But it is hardly an isolated item, since on 6 January 2018, when I last spent hours going through all the Putin wares on offer, CafePress said it had 1,930 Putin gift designs available on 251,000 products! While not all of these turned out to be exclusively about Putin, there were enough for anyone to get a solid sense of the American fascination with him. Moreover, as I noted in the last chapter, some of the CafePress designs still available for sale go back more than a decade – a fact that again speaks to the enduring attraction of the Russian leader.

Of course, the most wickedly sexualized satires are found on the material objects made during the 2016 US presidential election when Putin's perceived warm relationship with Donald Trump was used by people wanting to make political statements about the American candidate. Here, Putin serves as the perfect political counterpart, since his alpha-male credentials have been established in popular culture for at least a decade. It is worth remembering that in Russian political culture, as political scientist Valerie Sperling states, "undermining a political opponent's masculinity by implying his non-traditional sexual orientation is tantamount to stating that the man in question is more female than male and hence inferior."[12] The same dynamic exists in other parts of the world and in the United States, so objects that position Vladimir Putin lording it over his political opponents, thereby undermining their masculinities, are meant to seriously damage the reputations of the latter. The image on the sticker shown in figure 3.8 shows what I mean. The Russian president sits like a king on a throne while someone with the hair and fashion sense of Donald Trump kneels and fellates him. A further degree of control is implied by the placement of Putin's hand on the back of the Trump-figure's head, since it means Putin will control the pace of the implied motion as well as the depth of his penetration. Moreover, the pun in the caption brilliantly inverts the Republicans' obsession with Hillary Clinton's use of a private email server when she was secretary of state: "server" now implies that the new Republican president is in the thrall of his Russian counterpart instead.

Some of the items for sale online as the election campaign progressed were merely playful, such as a sticker showing both men in profile that humorously references the Lady Gaga song "Bad

3.8 Putin's Dedicated Private Server.

Romance," but whose caption changes the lyrics to "caught in a bad bromance." In another example, a T-shirt meant to look like a fake love letter from Putin to Trump – complete with a background lined like high school notebook paper and a fake kiss at the bottom – is amusingly suggestive, but still not blatantly sexualized.[13] Romance soon gives way to more explicit representations, however.

One of the most widely reproduced images of the Putin/ Trump bromance is usually referred to as "The Kiss." In May 2016, Dominykas Čečkauskas, who owns a Mexican restaurant in Vilnius (the capital of Lithuania), proudly unveiled a new mural on the outside of his establishment. The mural was the work of a local artist, Mindaugas Bonanu, and it showed Vladimir Putin locking lips with Donald Trump. The image evokes several iconic moments: from the kisses exchanged by Soviet and American soldiers when they met at the River Elbe in April 1945, to the "socialist fraternal kiss" exemplified by the famous photograph of Soviet leader Leonid Brezhnev and his East German counterpart Erich Honecker.[14] The latter was notably mocked by a piece of graffiti art painted on the remnants of the Berlin Wall by Dmitri Vrubel.[15] In Slavic cultures, a kiss on the lips is sometimes an acceptable greeting between men, but in the rest of the world – and particularly in the United States – such a kiss is read rather differently.[16] To an American viewer, the image implies that the relationship between Putin and Trump extended far beyond friendship and mutual admiration. The mural soon became a popular spot for people taking selfies, but the painting clearly did not please everyone. Within only a few months, in August 2016, vandals covered it up with white paint.[17]

What the vandals did not grasp was that it was already too late. Destroying the original painting did nothing to erase the image from popular consciousness. Indeed, it is doubtful that most of the people who have seen it even know where it originally came from. What mattered was that the image was already circulating far and wide across the internet, as all those print-on-demand services allowed the picture to be reproduced on every kind of textile product imaginable, on typical electoral kitsch like buttons and coffee mugs, and on accessories associated with modern technology. On Amazon.com, I bought a cell phone cover with "The Kiss" in September 2016. The seller, who was based in Lithuania, offered cases with the same design for literally every make and model of cell phone and tablet. A month later, I bought the men's underpants pictured in figure 3.9, also through Amazon. Interestingly, these were made by a company in British Columbia, Canada, but could only be bought on the US Amazon site. These two products, like so many of the objects I have already discussed, serve

3.9 "Make everything great again" men's underwear.

as a reminder that the nature and reach of Putin kitsch is truly global, even if my focus here is on the United States. They are evidence of how globalized the public political sphere has become.

The underpants are openly sexual. The Putin/Trump kiss is printed right in the middle of the backside and obviously evokes the expression "Kiss my ass." But, for viewers in the know, the underpants can also suggest ATM (ass to mouth) porn. Typically, in

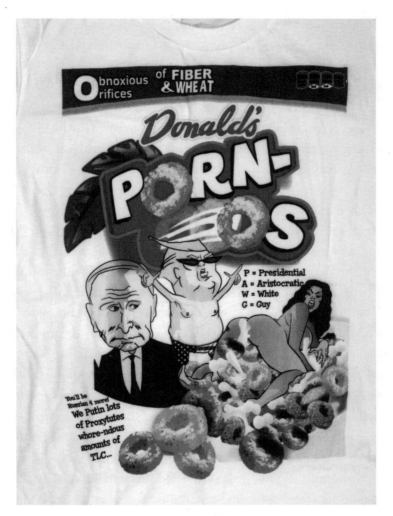

3.10 T-shirt advertising Donald's Porn-OOOs cereal.

ATM the participants have unprotected anal sex that is followed by one partner immediately fellating the other. The underlying message is that the person performing fellatio will have to "eat shit." "Feces is, in general, increasingly present in humiliation porn," according to Carmine Sarrachino and Kevin M. Scott's book on the pornographication of American culture. Still, I doubt even they expected to see it referenced in quite this way – on a piece of election kitsch featuring a US presidential candidate and the Russian president he often spoke so warmly about.[18]

The same region of the body is the focus of the "Donald's Porn-OOOs" cereal T-shirt that I bought on Etsy.com in November 2017 (fig. 3.10). Made by Dave, the owner of "UlmRocks" who according to Etsy lives in Ulm, Germany, the T-shirt was for some unknown reason mailed to me from Chatsworth, California, and the packing slip gave a return address of Charlotte, North Carolina. With so many things going on in this image, it is hard to know where to start talking about it. Mimicking the cover of a box of Fruit Loops, a popular sugary cereal for children, the information at the top of the design references the nutritional claims found on most North American cereals. But instead of giving actual information, the "obnoxious orifices of fiber and wheat" of this pornographied fake cereal claim to provide 100 per cent of your daily recommended needs of "sexy and senile," "tweety turd," and "climate cad," and the cereal claims to be "good at Russian into very bad things." Further down, boxer-short-clad Donald Trump stands next to a woman posed like a porn star.[19] His lack of clothing stands out as unusual for a depiction of a politician. Trump, especially, is known for the oversized red or blue power ties that go with his typical business suit uniform. Communications professor Hinda Mandell, whose research focuses on sex scandals in American politics, argues that removing the suit in essence removes the power from a politician: "he is stripped of his sartorial status and reduced to a man in his skivvies, harkening to the cultural trope – or nightmare – of appearing before a crowd in one's underwear."[20] For Trump's companion, the strategic covering of milk over parts of her anatomy does nothing to convey a sense of modesty. The milk on her breasts resembles a "money shot" – the moment when a man ejaculates on some part of his partner's body – which has been a standard feature of porn movies since the 1980s.[21] The milk running down her buttocks looks like semen leaking into the colourful cereal below. The reference there is to "creampies" – a term that refers to semen running out of someone's vagina or anus after their partner has just ejaculated into either orifice.[22] Cartoonists have been juxtaposing bodily functions and serious politics for centuries, so the image here fits into a long-standing tradition, and yet the use of a child's cereal box as the background seems to tap into something quite new.

A bemused – and fully dressed – Vladimir Putin looks on, taking in this entire scene. The image casts him in the role of pimp, which is not totally unbelievable given some of the rumours that still swirl as I write this book. In January 2018, a report in the *Wall Street Journal* alleged that Trump's lawyers had paid an adult film star $130,000 during the election campaign in order to cover up an alleged adulterous affair that occurred shortly after the candidate's wife had given birth to their son in 2006.[23] The Stormy Daniels story played out in the media for the rest of the year. But the words written below Putin on the shirt refer to another scandal involving the American president. Putin is supposed to have compromising information on the latter, information hinted at in a dossier compiled by Christopher Steele, who headed MI6's Russia station from 2004 to 2009.[24] It is alleged that Russian officials possess a tape of Trump cavorting with prostitutes in a Moscow hotel, and engaging in "golden showers."[25]

Golden showers, for those who may not know, are when someone urinates on another person for sexual pleasure. By January 2017 – in other words, right around inauguration time for the new American president – Twitter had roughly 70,000 jokes about the alleged incident.[26] CafePress had listings for stickers and fridge magnets that humorously mocked it as well. One of them, designed by "thealater" and uploaded to the site the day before the inauguration, was captioned "Tinkle tinkle little Czar, Putin put you where you are." Finally, almost a year later, with the scandal showing no sign of abating, someone calling himself Vladimirovich Platov published

3.11 BFF T-shirt.

an adult colouring book on the subject. According to the Amazon listing for *The PeePee Tape: Exclusive*, the colouring book "takes an exclusive look inside room 1101," and potential buyers are told to "grab your orange crayons and color the most controversial secret camera footage." So perhaps it is not surprising to find a reference to the affair on this shirt. The caption reads: "You'll be Russian 4 more! We Putin lots of Proxytutes whore-ndous amount of TLC."

Finally, just when you think it might be impossible to invoke another sexual fetish or kink for political reasons, there is the

BFF – "Best Friend Forever" – merchandise. Like the *Putin F*cks Trump* colouring book that opened the chapter, these items feature an invented Putin-Trump BDSM scene. The image was designed by one Lucas Hughes and uploaded to the CafePress website on 16 September 2016 (fig. 3.11). While I bought the T-shirt version, the same design is available on tote bags, drinking glasses, men's pajamas, and aprons – so on a vast array of everyday items. BDSM has become increasingly part of mainstream American culture in the past twenty years, but even viewers versed in or tolerant of it may be shocked by the way the image's implied political message is given here. "BDSM sexuality," in the words of cultural anthropologist Margot Weiss, "is supposed to be real, raw, and dirty, something that goes beyond the cleanly commodified, spectacular landscape, something that disrupts clear boundaries between privileged, normal sexuality and stigmatized, not normal sexuality."[27] This shirt turns a BDSM scene into a piece of banal Putin kitsch, albeit one that comes with a strong dose of political commentary. Far from feminizing Putin, who is after all dressed as a dominatrix, the picture emasculates his partner instead. The makers of the shirt use Putin's image as a weapon to imply that, as a man and as a political leader, Donald Trump has been metaphorically "pussy whipped." As was the case with so many other pieces of Putin kitsch that circulate in the globalized public sphere, the Russian remains powerful – the ultimate alpha male strutting his stuff on the world political stage.

The sexualized political kitsch that has been the focus of this chapter fits all of the parameters of pornographication. The items I have used as examples clearly show how images and references from the world of adult entertainment bled into the mainstream material culture one expects to encounter in election years, but then ventured into other categories such as children's toys. Double entendres abounded. References to the bodies of Donald Trump and Vladimir Putin, as well as imaginative reworkings of political slogans, were meant to provoke laughter. Most of that laughter came at the expense of Trump, whose masculinity was challenged by his submissive positioning vis-à-vis his Russian counterpart. Given how important constructions of masculinity are to American politics, and especially to the position of president, the objects presented here make a strong statement: they imply that Donald Trump is no match for Vladimir Putin and that he is not man enough to hold office.

4

What If...?

Vladimir Putin in American Fake Fiction

"This is a work of non-fiction from an alternate universe. Any persons, celebrities, politicians or public figures are not to be confused with any real persons from your universe." So reads the disclaimer at the start of *Air Force Two: Going Rogue*, a novel that imagines a world where John McCain and Sarah Palin won the 2008 US presidential election. The book, like the other texts that will be discussed in this chapter, is a piece of fake fiction.

What is fake fiction? Fake fiction has many of the hallmarks of fan fiction, a genre that predates the internet but blossomed with the internet's incorporation into everyday life.[1] In both genres, authors, who do not need to use their real names, can write pretty much whatever they want, since their texts are not mediated or altered by editors and publishing houses. Most fan fiction is posted to fan fiction websites (such as fanfiction.net or archiveofourown.org) and can be read for free; but works that I am calling fake fiction are self-published and sold, usually via Amazon.com. And whereas fan fictions, to quote professor

Rebecca Black, "are fan-created texts that are based on forms of popular culture such as books, movies, television, music, sports, and video games," fake fiction draws its characters from the political realm.[2]

In focusing on real people, fake fiction takes some aspects of RPS (real people slash), a subgenre of fan fiction where the stories "often tease out the relationship between the private and public self as they imagine a reality behind the celebrity persona" – but without the attention to detail that one usually sees in RPS.[3] In fan fiction, back-stories matter, since fans often know every single detail of characters' lives. Indeed, fans typically remember more than the actors who play the loved or loathed characters, or the writers who produce the original scripts. In fake fiction, only a smattering of truthful detail seems to be needed because the authors are more concerned with getting their political point across. That is because fake fiction is above all a political discourse. The people who write these texts demonstrate a deep interest in foreign affairs, and that matters more than, say, knowing the name of Vladimir Putin's current mistress. Still, real events are often only important because they serve as the starting point for "What would happen if…" fake fiction narratives.

In this chapter, I am admittedly stretching the definition of kitsch, which people typically associate with material objects. However, the connection between kitsch and books, even ones that only exist electronically, is not as far fetched as it seems. I think many people would view the graphic novel versions of literary classics such as *Crime and Punishment* and *Sense and Sensibility* as pieces of kitsch. (The latter has also been published in manga form, as has Shakespeare's *Romeo and Juliet*.) Certainly, the reworking of Jane Austen's novels to include vampires and zombies in the narratives has to fall under the banner of kitsch.[4] While the works that will feature in this chapter are in no way literary masterpieces, they do have an over-the-top quality that permeates their stories and that marks them as kitsch.

The trajectory of Putin fake fiction turns out to be quite similar to that of Putin material culture. The first Putin stories emerged when people wanted to offer opinions about Sarah Palin, which makes sense given how widely her remarks on Russia were reported in the news when she was running for vice-president. Palin's complete lack of foreign policy experience, and her rather limited knowledge of the rest of the world, could be deduced from her stance on Russia and then presented in a novel such as *Air Force Two: Going Rogue*. As one reviewer put it: "The book is a political hit job that uses the worst stereotypes that the left wants to believe."[5] Barack Obama's victory in the 2008 presidential election meant that Palin commentary evaporated, but new works soon emerged that pitted the president against his Russian counterpart. We have already seen how important contests of masculinity are to the image of an American president and how they figure in the discourse about his job performance. In Obama's case, his nemesis is often Vladimir Putin, whose alpha-male, James Bond villain credentials have long been established in popular culture. Fake fiction – like the short story *Putin and Obama in Russia*, which mocks Obama's handling of the Edward Snowden affair – offers another avenue to critique Obama's decisions.

The 2014 Russian invasion of Crimea brought a new kind of Putin fake fiction into the market. Now the Russian president's own actions were called into question, meaning that his image was not simply being used to undermine the reputation of other political figures. In *Putin Huylo and the Goldfish*, for instance, Russia's territorial ambitions vis-à-vis its neighbours are addressed. The story can be read as a warning to the rest of the world, since the author suggests that the acquisitive nature of Putin, and the advisors who egg him on, will never be satisfied. Without any kind of pushback against his demands, there will always be one more bit of land to seize.

Finally, in the past few years, an entire stream of sexually explicit fake fiction has emerged as people turn to pornographied texts to lambast their political leaders. Here I will only talk about *Hillary's Personal Emails: Secrets of State, Exposed (The Erotic International Politics of Sex)* and *Mission F@ck Putin*. (Because there are so many of them, I am saving the Trump/Putin stories for the next chapter.) Both of the stories that will be analyzed invent sexual encounters between Vladimir Putin and Hillary Clinton. Even though Clinton is presented as a worthy opponent for the wily Russian leader, she also comes across as somehow deviant and immoral. The authors convey that impression by including references to an array of fetishes – acts that they imply are not normal expressions of sexuality, particularly for a woman. Hence, the narratives are used to school the ambitious Clinton and undermine her status as a political figure.

On 19 October 2012, Jeff Pollard published *Air Force Two: Going Rogue* via Amazon Digital Services LLC. Pollard, according to his website, has a master's degree in screenwriting from the University of Missouri–Kansas City and has taught a class on "Discourse" there as an adjunct instructor for the Department of English.[6] Unfortunately, these credentials do not mean his 239-page book is particularly good or well-written; one Amazon reviewer used the word "juvenile" to describe its approach.[7] Still, the work does serve as an early example of Putin fake fiction and shows how references to the Russian leader crept into online American political discourse in much the same way that they appeared in material culture. In this case, a shirtless Putin is even included in the montage of photographs that make up the front cover of the book (fig. 4.1). The story is set in an alternative universe where John McCain won the 2008 US presidential election, making Sarah Palin the vice-president. She has been a disaster in that role – so much so that, as the next Republican convention approaches, McCain is determined to

4.1 Screenshot of the cover of *Air Force Two*.

dump her from his re-election ticket. When a particularly embarrassing public appearance by Palin at a high school in Alabama is skewered by the news media, McCain decides to send her abroad, thinking that a constant whirlwind of short trips will keep Palin busy and away from microphones in the United States. To sell the idea, Palin is told that she must go to Russia because McCain is not physically able to. "I'll go to Russia and show those godless, communist, liberal, feminist russkies how a real woman struts her stuff," a determined Palin vows.

Things do not look promising, however, because the next chapter opens with a real quotation from Palin's 24 September 2008 interview with Katie Couric. When asked whether Alaska's proximity to Russia may have given her some foreign policy experience, the candidate for America's second highest governmental position rather incoherently answered:

> Well, it certainly does because our ... our next door neighbors are foreign countries. They're in the state that I am the executive of. And there in Russia ... We have trade missions back and forth. We ... we do ... it's very important when you consider even national security issues with Russia as Putin rears his head and comes into the air space of the United States of America, where ... where do they go? It's Alaska. It's just right over the border. It is ... from Alaska that we send those out to make sure than an eye is being kept on this very powerful nation, Russia, because they are right there. They are right next to ... to our state.

Her words are not that different from the now infamous quotation that I mentioned two chapters ago. In both cases, Palin seemed to seriously underestimate her Russian rival and be blissfully unaware of how foreign policy actually works.

Putin, on the other hand, comes across in the novel as a Bond-style villain. In contrast to Palin, who spends much of this chapter of *Air Force Two* packing amidst all kinds of family drama, Putin, when the reader is first introduced to him, is lounging in bed. He has just enjoyed a sexual interlude with a gymnast whom Pollard calls Anastasia Gurevich.[8] As the woman leaves, Putin tells an aide that he is bored. He has done all kinds of stunts – here Pollard lists some memorable highlights that have established the real leader's public persona – and he has fixed the Russian economy. It seems he has no challenges left to face. The aide then suggests that Putin make sure he is in the Russian capital this coming week. Putin assumes that he is needed to have sex with the finalists in the Miss Russia pageant, and comments on his prowess with the opposite sex. But Putin is more excited when he learns that the aide had something else in mind. When the Russian leader is informed that Palin is due to visit for a brief photo-op with Prime Minister Dmitry Medvedev, he insists that a meeting with the American be set up for him as well.

The pair duly meet when Palin notices that a stop at the CSKA Ice Palace has been added to her itinerary. As Palin checks her iPad for information on the man she refers to as "Pootsy," she decides that he is a fellow political maverick, and, after seeing a picture of him without a shirt, a stud to boot. The pair enter the building to watch a hockey match. Over the next few pages, Pollard's version of Putin touches on many of the stereotypes people have of the Russian leader. He is said to have a steely gaze and that his KGB demeanor hides his emotions. At one point, Pollard writes, "Putin tries to smile, but he looks like a bear revealing his teeth." After drinking copious amounts of vodka, Putin and Palin go skating together once the hockey game ends. By then their small talk has turned into flirting. The scene suddenly jumps to the presidential yacht where Putin and Palin start to play the board game Risk. Putin frequently misses the various folksy expressions that pepper Palin's speech, so some serious miscommunications ensue. For instance, when Putin says he has heard that Palin is about to be replaced on the 2012 Republican ticket, Palin assumes they are talking about her husband Todd's possible infidelity. Palin's response – that she will get rid of her cheating spouse – is then taken by Putin to mean that Palin is about to launch a revolution for Alaskan independence and wants his support. All talk is shelved once the pair kiss and Putin carries the American vice-president into his bedroom.

While the book makes it clear that Putin and Palin have sex at this point, the reader is not given an exhaustive description of what their bodies do. As a result, Pollard's work is quite different from the pornographied texts that I will discuss at the end of this chapter. Here, sex is not really the point at all. It serves a narrative purpose only: it ensures that the plotlines about Alaskan independence, as well as the eventual Russian hijacking of a plane carrying Palin and her family, can move forward. The moment also allows the author to end the book with a mystery: when Palin announces in the final pages that she is pregnant, the omniscient narrator points out that the baby could have been fathered either by her husband, or Putin. But Putin himself almost totally disappears from the novel after chapter 4. He returns only briefly to share a phone call with Nancy Pelosi, when the latter arrives in the middle of the hijacking crisis at the Situation Room in Washington, DC.

In other words, Putin is more of a plot device than a central character in the novel. He appears because, on the campaign trail, most of Sarah Palin's most well-known gaffes concerning American foreign policy had to do with Russia. Her comments serve as the foundation for *Air Force Two*, for they allow Pollard to imagine an entire counterfactual narrative, starting with the premise, "What if McCain and Palin had won the election?" The apparent goal of the book is to suggest how awful such a scenario would have been. The references to Putin, who is cast in the role of an evil mastermind meddling in American affairs, only serve to underscore how ill-suited Palin was for the vice-presidency.

———•———

On 7 August 2013, President Barack Obama cancelled a summit that he was due to have in Moscow with Vladimir Putin the following month. Obama was reportedly furious over the Kremlin's decision a week earlier to grant asylum to former National Security Agency contractor Edward Snowden. Snowden, it will be remembered, leaked thousands of documents showing the American government had set up secret, mass surveillance programs to spy on its own, as well as some foreign, citizens. Articles outlining the contents of the documents began to appear in *The Guardian* newspaper in early June 2013. They sparked an international outcry and angered many US allies. Snowden viewed his action as a kind of civil disobedience – as something that he, as an international citizen, was morally compelled to do when confronted by the illegal behaviour of the US government.[9] However, to the American authorities he worked for, Snowden's behaviour was treasonous. The State Department revoked his passport and made it clear to other countries that they wanted Snowden returned to the United States to stand trial. Ironically, that allowed Vladimir Putin's government to add fuel to the fire. Arguing that the State Department's decision technically made Snowden a stateless person, the Russians deemed him a refugee and gave him new identity documents.[10] Eventually, Snowden also received a three-year residency permit. He remains in Russia today.

Joey Kaplan published his piece of fake fiction in the midst of the scandal. It appeared on the Amazon website on 18 July 2013 – in other words, after Snowden's revelations made him a wanted man, but before the Russians offered him permanent sanctuary. The six pages of *Putin and Obama in Russia* imagine a fake meeting between the two leaders at a Moscow airport. The text is structured more like a play than a short story, and the invented dialogue actually reads a bit like a sketch that could have been performed by the Three Stooges. Upon arrival, Barack Obama immediately asks for Edward Snowden to be turned over as promised in an earlier phone call. Putin, who refers to his American counterpart as "my little servant," then proceeds to ask for an ever-growing list of things before he hands over the fugitive. Kaplan starts with rings. He is referencing an incident from 2005 when Putin tried on a Super Bowl ring belonging to New England Patriots owner Robert Kraft and allegedly slipped it into his pocket. That story broke in the US media in mid-June 2013, and the ring has apparently never been returned to Kraft.¹¹ Kaplan's Putin demands Obama's wedding and presidential rings. Seeing his nemesis turn them over spurs Putin to ask for the keys to Air Force One, as well as the American president's passport and wallet. Once Putin has all of these things, Snowden duly appears, but only via video chat to say hello to the two leaders. Obama's efforts to secure him have been foiled, while Putin, who is again cast in the role of evil genius, gloats about how well he came out of their deal.

The goal here is clearly to make the outfoxed Obama look powerless and inept. In that, the story is reminiscent of the material objects that cast the relationship between the two presidents as a confrontational competition. If someone dislikes the American president and feels that he is not living up to the masculinized standards of his office, stories such as this one provide a way to express those sentiments and potentially reach a wide audience in the process.

A different kind of kleptomania drives the narrative of our next piece of fake fiction. Here, in *Putin Huylo and the Goldfish*, Putin does not amass material objects, but is driven to add more and more territory to Russia. The story was uploaded to Amazon.com on 11 March 2016. Its author, listed as Bacillus Bulgaricus, explains his use of a pseudonym in the introduction. Readers are told that he is a Bulgarian politician who wants to make sure his dislike of Putin is not deemed the official position of his government, but who still feels compelled to let the world know that not all of his countrymen are pro-Russian. As if this statement was not enough to establish the author's political opinions, the book is dedicated to Boris Nemtsov, the liberal Russian politician who was an ardent critic of Vladimir Putin and who was gunned down in Moscow on 27 February 2015.

And I have not even mentioned the title yet. "Putin khuylo!" is an expression used in both Russian and Ukrainian that can be translated as "Putin is a dickhead," although the words "dickwad" or "prick" fit just as well. It was first used as a chant by fans of the FC Metalist Kharkiv on the eve of the Russian annexation of Crimea, but soon fans of other clubs adopted the slogan and recordings of it being sung were posted on YouTube.[12] After that, the expression spilled over into mainstream Ukrainian rock music and was used by several Ukrainian politicians, something which provoked the ire of Russian officials.[13] Memes and material culture played a big role in spreading the expression around the world.[14] Not since the globalized public sphere reacted negatively to Russia's 2013 ban on what the country's leaders referred to as LGBTQ propaganda targeting minors had so much overtly anti-Putin material flooded the internet – although it must be admitted that the American response to the Russian invasion of Crimea was somewhat mixed. Official government statements deplored the move and deemed it an illegal act of aggression vis-à-vis another sovereign state. Yet television coverage, particularly that of Fox News, contained tinges of admiration for Putin's boldness, even as reports decried the invasion itself. Fox commentators used the moment to contrast Putin's leadership style with that of President Obama; whereas the former was praised for his decisiveness, the latter was considered weak and ineffective.[15] In both of these cases, however, Russian policies were engaged with directly via internet writings and material culture, and in these arenas Vladimir Putin came in for some harsh criticism. The materials that were created deviated from the pattern we typically see with Putin kitsch, for they did not use the Russian leader's image to comment on the abilities of others. Instead, the harsh spotlight of political criticism was turned squarely on Putin alone.

Putin Huylo and the Goldfish is a satirical reworking of "The Tale of the Fisherman and the Fish," a fairy tale in verse by one of Russia's most beloved writers, Alexander Pushkin. The story takes Vladimir Putin's well-known love of fishing – it is worth remembering that his summer holidays frequently involve fishing in Siberian rivers – and uses it against him. "Hopefully, my modern interpretation of the tale will inspire many free-thinking people in Russia and around the world to question the legitimacy of Russian nationalistic myths," the author writes, before adding that these myths have been used to "justify the occupation of Ukrainian and Georgian territories and the imprisonment of innocent critics of Putin's regime."

The tale begins when Putin catches a Russian-speaking goldfish. When the fish begs to be released, Putin, to the surprise of his entourage, complies with its wish. The lackeys flatter their boss before encouraging him to ask the fish for a favour in return for its freedom. "O Putin, o Huylo," they say, "you are indeed the greatest ruler of our homeland. Nobody else could be so just and generous with our great nation. You always make sure that the stores are full with reasonably priced vodka and potatoes. You never miss an opportunity to give the war veterans another medal instead of decent pensions. You control the media so tightly that you never have to worry about public opinion." Putin takes their words to heart and asks the fish for Abkhazia and South Ossetia, two pieces of disputed territory in the Caucasus that the Russians have been interested in since the collapse of the Soviet Union.[16] The pattern continues, with Putin's minions encouraging him to ask for more and more land, including the Crimean Peninsula and the Donbass region of Ukraine. Their flattery invokes several familiar aspects of Putin's image along the way. At one point, they say, "You never miss an opportunity to appear in the media half-naked holding a gun to show how strong you are!" Putin's diplomatic skills are also praised. "You know how to lie successfully to naïve Western diplomats and heads of state," his lackeys tell the Russian president as they encourage him to ask the fish for a Eurasian Economic Union.

Finally, the greed of Putin's entourage brings the situation to an end. Their rather over-the-top demand that the fish make Russia the world's only superpower, as well as that the fish become a Russian citizen and work directly under Putin's orders, is too much. The fish ignores Putin and swims away. When Putin returns home, he finds that all of the gains he secured are now lost. "Only the Russians who did not manage to immigrate," the author tells us, "continued to drink cheap vodka waiting for the next speech of their favorite dictator Putin Huylo." The moral of the story is, of course, that Putin's – and by extension Russians' – aggressive territorial ambitions will be unsuccessful in the long run. Those lands cannot be held forever, and Russia will only lose allies if the country continues to behave in this fashion.

————•————

A year after the invasion of Crimea, references to Vladimir Putin began to creep into discussions of the upcoming American presidential election. The two pieces of fake fiction that I will talk about here – *Hillary's Personal Emails: Secrets of State, Exposed (The Erotic International Politics of Sex)* by Trashcan Jones, and *Mission F@ck Putin* by Nick Beyond – use explicit sex to revisit many familiar criticisms of Hillary Clinton as she ran for the nation's highest office. The texts have an ironic undertone, of course, because the relationship between Clinton and Putin is a particularly acrimonious one. In 2008, then senator Clinton was heard joking about former president George W. Bush's comment that he had gotten a glimpse of the Russian leader's soul when they met at a summit in Slovenia in 2001. Clinton said that was impossible because the former KGB agent does not have one.[17] Two years later, when Clinton visited Moscow, the pair had an uncomfortable meeting, followed by a press conference where Putin launched into a litany of complaints about American policies towards Russia. Later, Putin blamed Clinton when protestors took to the streets in Moscow in December 2011 to show their displeasure with Russia's election results. Putin's hackles had been raised after Clinton issued a statement indicating that she believed there had been widespread fraud and vote-rigging. In fact, Clinton took a hard line on Russia throughout her tenure as secretary of state, and it is fair to say that she and Putin loathe each other. In other words, there is no one less likely to have a sexual relationship with Hillary Clinton than Vladimir Putin, which makes the scenario a perfect "what if...?"

Unfortunately for Clinton, Americans have been making jokes and innuendos about her sex life for more than twenty years. Given that Hillary Clinton's ambitions obviously extended far beyond the traditional roles of first ladies – namely, to be wives and mothers – one way for critics to chastise her for those desires was to attack her femininity. In the 1990s, for instance, political cartoonists regularly suggested that she had usurped the pants in her marriage and was in fact running the country instead of her husband. The emasculated president, in some images, was depicted wearing a dress or carrying a purse.[18] A significant number of cartoons also posited that the Clintons somehow did not have a normal marriage by showing the couple reading policy documents in bed rather than enjoying any romantic time together. Such drawings implied that Hillary Clinton was not a desirable or exemplary woman. Moreover, since Clinton was "held up as the representative feminist," in the words of professor Charlotte Templin, she could be "used as a stick to beat feminism and to scapegoat feminism for various ills of the modern world."[19]

By running for a Senate seat as her husband's time in the Oval Office drew to a close, Hillary Clinton ensured that she remained at the centre of American politics. This also meant that she continued to be subjected to sexually charged rhetoric. Indeed, things only seemed to get worse on that score. Several moments in the run-up to the 2008 presidential election clearly bear the hallmarks of outright pornographication, according to Karrin Anderson's framework (mentioned in the last chapter). All concerned the use of the word "cunt" in connection with Clinton, who was being criticized for being too ambitious and for not abiding by traditional gender norms. According to Anderson, the "subtext of these examples is, of course, that any woman who seeks the office of U.S. president is unnatural, dangerous, even deviant."[20]

Fast forward a few years into another presidential election cycle, and we find that not only have references to explicit sexuality become more widespread in political commentary, but such comments are also venturing into new media. Back in 2008, most of those "cunt" references vis-à-vis Clinton came on television, with the exception of the logo printed onto T-shirts for the anti-Clinton "Citizens United Not Timid" political action committee. In the 2016 election, as we have seen, all kinds of material goods tapped pornographic elements in order to offer political opinions. Not surprisingly, fake fiction did too.

"This is a work of satire." This clarification is printed on the copyright page of *Hillary's Personal Emails: Secrets of State, Exposed (The Erotic International Politics of Sex)*, although it is unlikely that any reader would mistake the thirty-seven-page story for a real episode in the relationship between Hillary Clinton and Vladimir Putin. With that said, like many works of fake fiction, the opening few pages of the story have just enough factual information to make it seem possible. Obviously referencing the never-ending saga of missing emails and Clinton's use of a private computer server, the text was published via Amazon Digital Services LLC on 12 March 2015. The author, who uses the pseudonym Trashcan Jones, creates a fake email exchange between the pair, and one can see why either would want the messages to disappear, given that they delve into more and more sexual fetishes as they go on.[21]

Clinton sends the first message, conveying her excitement to the Russian leader that he will be visiting the United States. Putin's reply – informing her that he will be making a speech at the United

Nations in New York – foreshadows a real moment, since Putin did, in fact, address the UN General Assembly on 28 September 2015. He then reminds the secretary of state of the fun they supposedly had in his suite with a collection of sex toys when they were both in Oslo, Norway. The opportunity the author is referring to came in early November 1999 when Putin had a testy meeting with US president Bill Clinton.[22] Over the next several messages Putin tells Clinton what he would like her to wear when they next see each other, and the pair go on to outline the smorgasbord of sex acts they will engage in. Oral sex will apparently lead to anal sex, with a dildo-strapped Clinton assuming the dominant position. While talking about this scenario, fake Putin throws in a few sentences signalling his partner's political importance. "My entire body submits to your dominance as I scream into my pillow," he writes. "You are the most powerful woman in the world. I am yours." Yet, at the last minute, the story's author pulls back slightly from this depiction of a totally dominant Hillary Clinton. Instead, the narrative concludes with another message from Clinton fantasizing about Putin's semen shooting into her eyes and all over her breasts, thereby reversing the power dynamic of the scene to a small extent. With that, the story comes to an end.

Even more fluids and fetishes feature in Nick Beyond's story, *Mission F@ck Putin*. Published via Amazon Digital Services LLC on 3 February 2016, the twenty-two-page tale is full of grammatical errors and bad prose. It also contains some rather mixed political messages. The front cover image shows Vladimir Putin giving the reader the finger (fig. 4.2). When I saw that, I assumed the work would feature a dominant Putin, but I was wrong. The story instead presents a Putin who is physically unimpressive, racist, erratic, and addicted to cocaine. Hillary Clinton, on the other hand, simply dominates everyone around her. That is consistent with one of the comments the author makes before the story starts. "Mrs. Hillary is a very strong woman and politic [*sic*] person," he writes in the

4.2   Screenshot of cover of *Mission F@ck Putin.*

preface. "So I believe that she has been doing a lot for America." Readers are about to find out just how far Clinton is willing to go for her country.

The first chapter opens with a furious Vladimir Putin ranting to advisors such as Foreign Minister Sergei Lavrov about Russian relations with the West. He pauses only long enough to snort several lines of coke from a diamond-encrusted box and to order an attack on Ukraine. Once he has calmed down, the Russian leader visits Patriarch Kirill of Moscow, whom he refers to as a "pimp." The references to Lavrov and the patriarch are typical of fake fiction, in the sense that they offer a veneer of real detail that reveals the political engagement of the author, but do not stop him from then wandering off into fantasy land.

Hillary Clinton makes her entrance in the next chapter. Her morning routine is interrupted by a call from President Obama. At a meeting later that day, Obama and John Brennan (who served as the director of the CIA from March 2013 to January 2017) tell Clinton they have a spy in the Kremlin and argue that Russia cannot be allowed to occupy Ukraine. After consuming copious amounts of whisky, the inebriated trio come up with a plan they call "fuck Putin." The remaining pages of the story apparently show that plan being carried out while Clinton, for no reason, also has sex with a Russian agent named Ivan before seducing Putin himself. I say "apparently" because nowhere are readers actually given a description of the plan, and there are some sideline elements – such as Clinton having a special poison to use on the Russian leader – that are mentioned but not fully developed. Moreover, the story has no real resolution, since nothing tangible is gained from the Russian leader in the wake of his interlude with Clinton. Perhaps the sole purpose of her visit is to literally "fuck Putin" so that her American bosses can laugh about it? In other words, is attacking Putin's masculinity, the core of his public persona, enough?

Certainly, Putin the sex symbol is nowhere to be found during his encounter with Clinton in the Kremlin dining room. Instead, readers are told, "Putin stood in front of her naked and depressed. His flabby body, grown slightly fat from a luxury life, was trembled [sic]. Balding forehead was covered with perspiration." Clinton is the aggressor throughout: she rips Putin's shirt to use as a gag; she handcuffs him and beats him with a belt; and she sodomizes the Russian leader with her finger and a container of lubricant. After putting a dog collar and leash on the still-handcuffed Putin, Clinton inserts a candle into his anus. The author suggests that Putin enjoys being penetrated in this way because he ejaculates on the floor. After removing the handcuffs, Clinton proceeds to walk Putin like a dog to a nearby toilet. Once the pair have arrived, Putin is ordered to put his mouth over Clinton's vagina while she urinates; he is told to swallow and then lick her clean. Finally, after they have returned to the dining room, Clinton straps on a large black dildo (described as a present from Obama) and proceeds to use it on Putin. After penetrating him for several minutes, Clinton rearranges their bodies so that she can shove the dildo into her partner's mouth until he vomits. She is said to be so aroused by the sight that she has an orgasm. Clinton leaves Putin sprawled on the floor in a puddle of mixed bodily fluids. The author then simply says that she returned to her hotel room to clean up before leaving Russia on the first available plane.

Texts like this tap into an assumed binary where BDSM and sexual fetishes are considered abnormal. According to cultural anthropologist Margot Weiss, such "representations reinforce boundaries between normal and not normal by allowing the viewer to consume a bit of the kinky other while buttressing the privilege, authority, and essential normalcy of the self."[23] So, in other words, by suggesting that Hillary Clinton and Vladimir Putin engage in "deviant" sex, the author of our piece of fake fiction can reinforce the supposed values of the mainstream while simultaneously impugning the political reputations of his characters. He implies that Putin is not the capable alpha male that his public image would suggest, and that Clinton, who so dramatically defies traditional gender norms and usurps male authority in the story, is not an acceptable political figure either. However, the growing visibility of BDSM in mainstream popular culture makes some of what the author is trying to do banal rather than naughty. Hence, *Mission F@ck Putin* winds up being both a commentary on US-Russian relations and a piece of kitsch.

"Hopefully, my modern interpretation of the tale will inspire many free-thinking people in Russia and around the world to question the legitimacy of Russian nationalistic myths which justify the occupation of Ukrainian and Georgian territories and the imprisonment of innocent critics of Putin's regime." With these words, the author of *Putin Huylo and the Goldfish* sums up the goal of his invented narrative. Not surprisingly, it is a political one. Political engagement is at the very root of the genre I define as fake fiction. While drawing on some of the conventions of fan fiction, fake fiction spins its stories around the actions of politicians and world leaders. The authors generally include just enough detail drawn from actual events and policies to give their works a kernel of veracity before they venture off into the "what if" realm. Because the stories are self-published, there is no outside force to mediate the political opinions being expressed – or, it must be said, to improve the quality of the writing.

Putin features in these works in two ways. On occasion, fake fiction addresses Russian actions directly, most notably the 2014 invasion of the Crimean Peninsula. But most of the time Putin's image serves as a foil for American politicians. His out-manoeuvring of Sarah Palin demonstrates how ill-suited she was for the position of American vice-president, and, given that *Air Force Two* ends with the US facing a Russian invasion in support of Alaskan independence, how dangerous electing her might have been. President Obama does not fare well in contests with Vladimir Putin either. As was the case with the material objects we have already looked at, in fake fiction Obama is no match for his Russian rival. In *Putin and Obama in Russia*, for instance, we see the American being outwitted as he attempts to deal with the aftermath of the Edward Snowden affair. Yet again, Putin comes across as a stereotypical arch-villain in a political thriller, only in this case there is no happy ending because the US president does not save the day and recover the traitorous spy. Instead, in only six pages the author manages to undermine Obama's presidential masculinity. By contrast, it is the femininity of Hillary Clinton that is called into question in the pieces of fake fiction that show her having an imagined sexual relationship with Putin. Unlike Obama, the devious and cunning Clinton is shown to be willing to use nefarious means to best the Russian, but that does not mean she is depicted in a positive light. An unspoken binary – where sexual fetishes are not considered normal – is evoked. By exhaustively listing the sex acts in which Clinton and Putin engage, the authors of these pornographied texts work to discredit both parties. As we shall see, a similar dynamic is at work when writers consider the perceived bromance between Vladimir Putin and Donald J. Trump, which is the subject of the next chapter.

5

Holding Out for a Hero
Slashing the Trump-Putin Bromance

"Soon the smell of sweat, spray tan and megalomania filled the air." That sentence, taken from Will Smut's *Putin It in Trump*, is my favourite line from a piece of Trump/Putin slash. A genre of fan fiction, slash stories and novels are created when fans perceive a homoerotic subtext in a relationship between two heterosexual men. The first slash writings emerged in the mid-1970s when fans of *Star Trek* began to create Kirk/Spock narratives, but other buddy pairings derived from television (such as Starsky/Hutch) also sparked viewers' creativity.[1] Since then, the amount of slash in circulation has mushroomed, fed in large part by the expansion of the internet. As fan writings shifted online, some of them also changed in nature. When slash began, it was taboo to write about real people, or to get any kind of financial reward for one's work.[2] Those guidelines eroded in the twenty-first century as people began posting more and more slash about celebrities and politicians. These stories are categorized as RPS ("real people slash"), and authors use factual information from their subjects' biographies as well as real-world occurrences to ground their narratives. They often produce very nuanced depictions; as one scholar put it, "RPS narratives present celebrities as fully formed, intricate, and interesting characters, in opposition to their often one-dimensional media portrayals."[3] The Trump/Putin stories that will be discussed in the coming pages mimic real people slash, in that they argue that sex is fundamental to understanding the relationship between the two men. But their authors are less concerned with getting backstories and details right, and more concerned with politics. As a result, slashers are publishing works that are, in the words of an Amazon.com review of *Mr. Trump Meets Mr. Putin* posted by "Ted P." on 19 October 2016, "part biting political satire, part absurd dystopian future, and [at least in the eyes of some readers] completely funny."

The first pieces of Donald Trump erotic fiction were listed for sale on Amazon.com less than six weeks after he announced his candidacy in the US presidential election. From that point on, and continuing past his inauguration in January 2017, dozens of titles were written and self-published. They included *Thump the Trump Rump!* by Tea Bagger, a trilogy called *Donald Feels the Bern* by Cliff Fuxtable, and *Trump Temptation: The Billionaire and the Bellboy* by Elijah Daniel. This last story exposed the genre to the world because reporter Alison Flood wrote about it for *The Guardian* newspaper.[4] Some of the works – like the Bernie Sanders trilogy I just mentioned or *Trump and Pence: Passion in the White House* by M. Erika – feature other notable politicians, so they offer a political critique alongside their satirization of Donald Trump's sexuality. The stories are not really meant to arouse. Instead, their authors use explicit sex and a whole host of fetishes to undermine the credibility of political leaders and suggest in a roundabout way that they are not suitable to lead.[5] Narratives of the Trump/Putin relationship are at the forefront of this discourse, since they far outnumber the texts devoted to other politicians – with the possible exception of those about Hillary Clinton. Trump/Putin slash demonstrates the extent to which the perceived relationship between the two men has captured the attention of the public and how the Russian president again serves as a foil for his American counterpart.

Week after week during the 2016 election campaign, Donald Trump and Vladimir Putin made complimentary remarks about each other and suggested that they were keen to meet in person as soon as possible. The focus on the men's relationship is emblematic of the current media landscape, which simplifies foreign policy, in particular, to personalized contests between national leaders.[6] In such contests, masculinity matters, and it is the performance of masculinity that some slashers attack in their writings. Since Vladimir Putin already had a well-established sexualized public image, it did not require mental gymnastics to turn him into a slash hero. Trump's antics on the campaign trail and during his first year in office were also well-suited to extreme parody. In addition, the pornographication of American political culture in the past decade or so made slash an acceptable venue for attacking the new US president.

This chapter looks closely at eleven pieces of Trump/Putin slash to show what common features and themes crop up when writers turn to slash as a form of political commentary. The texts are often quite compatible with the public image that Putin has crafted for the past decade. For instance, Putin's love of the outdoors, tendency to be photographed without half of his clothes, and physical strength are noted frequently. Slash writers have no trouble fitting him into a paradigm of "frontier masculinity," where leaders test themselves in harsh climates at the geographic fringes of their countries. Putin's alpha-male qualities in these scenarios only serve to underscore what the slash producers see as Trump's failings as a leader and as a man.

That is also evident in how the two men's bodies are written about. Putin's pectoral muscles are fetishized constantly – as they are in material culture – and his penis is assigned magical qualities. By contrast, Trump's undersized member fails to impress, and he cannot control his bodily emissions. When it comes to sexual acts between the two men, Putin is usually the dominant figure. It should be noted that positioning is very important to the political messages that the stories are trying to make. "Topping" – in other words, the sexual act of penetrating another man – signifies the dominance of one man over another, and confirms rather than denies the masculinity of the dominant partner.[7] The Russian president's reputation has long relied on this notion of dominance. Political scientist Valerie Sperling notes that "a significant element of Putin's machismo … rests on his assertion of power over other men – from state officials and economic powerhouses to journalists and foreign diplomats."[8] Consequently, slash texts can play with ingrained sexism and homophobia. The latter, when used as a political tool, "relies on the involuntary rescinding of someone's masculinity, thereby 'feminizing' the man and reducing his social authority."[9] By generally making Trump the bottom in his couplings with Putin, the notion that Putin is a strong man is reinforced, while the American leader is mocked mercilessly for his pretensions.

Finally, Trump/Putin slash suggests that Trump will denigrate and disgrace the office that he holds. It does so in a carnivalesque fashion by evoking a host of symbols of state, like the American flag, in deliberately offensive ways. The meanings of American rituals of power, such as the presidential inauguration or the hosting of state dinners, are similarly inverted when slash writers create alternative possibilities – ones where the US president is not in control of the events or even of his own body. Finally, by setting some of the most explicit scenes in sacred spaces – sometimes the Kremlin, more often the White House – works of Trump/Putin slash imply that Trump cannot govern his country by himself. Instead, the Russian president is literally and metaphorically at the centre of American politics today.

A significant component of Vladimir Putin's public image involves his supposed mastery of the Russian physical landscape. In a seemingly endless series of publicity stunts, as well as during his annual vacations to some of his country's most out-of-the-way locations, the man has been transformed into a modern-day Tarzan. As some scholars have noted, Putin does appear more comfortable around animals than people.[10] His affection for his black lab, Koni, is also well known. The irony is, of course, that Putin signed a decree eliminating the Russian federal environmental protection agency early in his time in office. Still, Putin's image-makers are not going to let a small thing like that stop them from presenting the president as "the husband of Russia's entire natural world," to quote historian Tatiana Mikhailova.[11] Instead, they conceive of ever more exotic adventures for Putin – everything from putting satellite transmitter collars on a Siberian tiger and a polar bear to flying a hang-glider to lead the migration of a flock of storks. While the over-the-top theatrics of these moments no doubt lead to much eye-rolling and even the desire to debunk their constructed nature, the fact still remains that the underlying premise – that Putin is king of the natural world – is conveyed to the public.[12]

Indeed, the mastery of nature is instrumental to Putin's brand of masculinity. He is tapping into a long-running cultural code that is recognizable not just in Russia, but throughout much of the Western world, where taming the frontier is also associated with political leadership and state control. Remember that both Ronald Reagan and George W. Bush successfully played up the cowboy angle during their presidencies, and Canadian prime minister Stephen Harper insisted upon leading annual military exercises in the Arctic from 2006 to 2013. The behaviours of all three men fit within the parameters of "frontier masculinity." When scholars use that term, they are suggesting that "remote spaces such as the Arctic are often framed as 'testing places' that invite men (often white and hailing from elsewhere) to exercise their endurance, innovation, and strength."[13] Putin certainly seems to think so, since he has been keen to test his body in Russia's most rugged terrains. Having cameras along to record the moments only ensures that the rest of the world also recognizes his alpha-male credentials.

Slash fiction has taken up this part of Putin's image as well. Sometimes it is only referred to in passing, as in *Excess of Evil: An Alternatively Factual Trump/Putin Romance*, where the Russian president keeps two tigers as pets. (His "comfort animal" in the *Adventure Buddies* colouring book mentioned in chapter 2 was also a tiger.) Two other stories use more detailed references to Putin the dog lover to make their political point, although it must be admitted that they remove the actual canine to do so. In *Back-Door Politics: Volume 1 of the Memoirs of Donald Trump as Told to His Best Friend*, for example, Putin strokes Trump's belly like a dog and uses the endearment "Little Cub" when speaking to his American counterpart. The scenario obviously displays Putin's dominance over Trump, but also dehumanizes and ridicules the latter. The same notions are conveyed more directly in *Putin on the Trump*, a story that imagines the two men as college roommates. There the dominant figure – Putin – has Trump sit on the floor at his feet like a dog and eventually perform oral sex on the Russian in that position. All the while, Putin commends Trump, saying, "Good boy, doggy capitalist." Nor is the dog imagery forgotten as the story moves on to other subjects. At the very end of the narrative, after both men have become presidents of their respective countries, Trump visits his old flame in Moscow. After a night of sexual hijinks that includes Putin spanking his lover and Trump licking the Russian's anus, Trump wakes up in a doggy bed in Putin's private rooms. Both narratives, literally and figuratively, turn Trump into "Putin's bitch," thereby undermining the masculinity and political legitimacy of the American while at the same time conforming with the prevailing impression of Putin.

In terms of the other stories, frontier masculinity comes through most strongly in Lester Moorehead's *Putin the Moves on Trump*, since almost every aspect of the story references it in some way. The narrative opens with Trump flying over the Arctic wilderness of Siberia and deciding that he wants to build an ice hotel. Unfortunately, mid-flight he fires everyone on board, and when they parachute off the plane the hapless American is stranded. Not surprisingly, the plane crashes.

But all is not lost, because a hero is about to save the day. It turns out that Putin is embarking on an annual ritual – what the author refers to as "the yearly Mother Russia versus Mother Nature Ceremony where the leader of Russia must prove the dominance of the Russian spirit over the Russian wilderness." The book's third chapter opens with Putin in a helicopter flying over the same landscape as Trump. The Russian strips off his flight suit, covers his body in a mixture of polar bear blubber and borscht, and leaps from the chopper. Landing on top of a family of rabbits, the thrifty and resourceful Putin immediately skins them to make fur underwear and shoes. He then engages a bear in combat, but the animal is no match for Putin's judo skills. Clearly referencing the kinds of images found in material culture, the defeated bear becomes Putin's primary mode of transportation in the remainder of the novel. But the ludicrousness does not stop there. Instead, the author gives Putin the skills of a superhero: he fells trees merely by running into them and he karate chops them into the logs to build a cabin. By the end of his first day in the wild, the Russian leader has all the shelter he needs to survive in the harsh Siberian landscape.

The contrast with Trump is striking. The American does not even realize the danger he is in when the wreckage of his plane is surrounded by a pack of wolves. Instead, he is too busy mourning the loss of his cell phone. It is Putin who steps in to drive the wolves away. A child-like Trump then weeps for his phone on the Russian's chest before being rocked to sleep. This kind of scene may remind readers of a common Trump/Putin meme that has been reproduced on a number of objects and was used as the cover for Avell Kro's *The Adventures of Trutin and Pump*, a piece of fake fiction like the ones that were featured in the last chapter (fig. 5.1).

5.1 Putin holds baby Trump. Meme printed onto a campaign-style button.

Trump stumbles back into danger a few pages later, when he wanders through the forest pretending that the trees are people he can fire. Lacking a phone but still needing to feed his Twitter addiction, Trump breaks a branch off a tree and uses it to write mean tweets in the snow. He is so distracted that he does not notice the arrival of the wolf pack. Yet again, Putin arrives in the nick of time to save his charge, and this time Trump is aroused by the Russian leader's masculine display. He fondles Putin's penis as the men ride the bear out of harm's way, and Trump's arousal only grows when he learns what Putin has been up to in his absence. Putin, it seems, has not been content to laze away the day, but rather has built an ice castle for Trump.

Putin's masculine performance fits with the image that has been created for him since the first batch of shirtless photographs of him was released. His actions also stimulate Trump, who responds by begging the hyper-masculine Russian to have sex with him, which allows the author to further emasculate Trump, metaphorically speaking. The ensuing passage mocks Trump's blustery way of speaking and habit of bragging about his own capabilities by putting these words in his mouth: "Oh, I can take it. I'm the world's greatest power bottom. I'll take that whole monster cock and then some. Try and get those balls in there, too. No one can take a dick up the ass like the old Trumpster!" The assumption here is that bottoms are less powerful in homosexual pairings, which admittedly is an old-fashioned and rather homophobic notion.[14] Indeed, the whole Trump/Putin genre has been labelled homophobic by a number of commentators.[15]

I am not going to quibble with their interpretations, but I tend to assume that people who write slash about politicians are trying to use their own views against them. That certainly works in the cases of Putin and Trump, since neither of them is a supporter of LGBTQ rights. Moreover, as I mentioned in earlier chapters, for several hundred years people have created politicized pornography, which hinged upon criticizing public figures by depicting them engaged in sexually explicit acts said to deviate from the norm. The deliberate melding of sex and politics is particularly evident in two quotations from a different story: Bryce Chadwell's *Excess of Evil*. There, as Putin begins to penetrate the new American president with his penis, the author writes that "Trump buckled his hips and shook against Putin, which only spurred Putin further to quench his need to conquer. Ukraine was just a dry run. He had chided China. He had slow-roasted Turkey. Now, with The President trapped in his place of power, he would exact absolute control over the free world." In other words, Chadwell sexualizes the entirety of Putin's foreign policy. Trump's response also contains politicized elements, but these reflect the ways in which Trump performs in front of cameras in the

US. "Trump stiffened at the intrusion, and tried to avoid Putin's dick the way he avoided interview questions: by slapping the air, mentioning imaginary approval ratings, and curling into a defensive fetal position while blaming Obama." In the end – and I think this is the point of the scene, as well as of the texts in general – neither man comes across as an ideal political leader.

———•———

The fascination with Putin's pectoral muscles that we saw in American material culture carries over into slash narratives. In these texts, Putin's physique matches that of the heroes found in conventional romance novels and then some. The front cover of *Putin on the Trump* is a good case in point (fig. 5.2). In that story, where the two men meet as students at the Wharton School at the University of Pennsylvania, Trump's immediate sexual attraction to his new roommate, foreign exchange student Putin, is signified by the fact that he is fascinated by the movement of the Russian's sweaty pecs as the young man runs across campus. Trump is sufficiently aroused that he eventually uses the sweat that he gets on his hands after inadvertently touching Putin's chest as a lubricant when he masturbates in a washroom.

Watching a shirtless Putin undulate his pectoral muscles stimulates Trump in *Putin the Moves on Trump* as well. Finally, Putin's chiselled chest features in *Pootin on the Tramp: Tremendous Erotica, the Best Erotica* by A Sultry Citizen. In that story, Putin visits the new president at the White House because he is angered by intelligence saying that Trump has been having sex with someone else. Trying to catch Trump in the act, Putin lifts up his desk – only to find that Donald is actually getting a blow job from his daughter Ivanka – and in the process, Putin's shirt is shredded by his bulging muscles. This eye-rolling detail is reminiscent of countless scenes featuring Marvel's Incredible Hulk or the moment in the

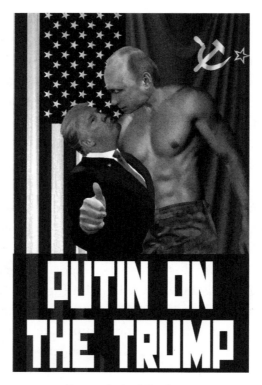

5.2 Screenshot of the front cover
of *Putin on the Trump*.

film *Furious 7* when Dwayne Johnson simply flexes his muscles to break the plaster cast that encases his arm. In other words, the Russian president is equated with the fictional action heroes who populate American movie screens.

However, because the texts that I am discussing are works of slash fiction, they do not stop with bulging muscles and the destruction of clothing. And because they are not subject to government ratings systems, they can be far more explicit when they discuss Putin's body. We see that in all the references to what I refer to as Putin's magic penis. First of all, in contests of masculinity, particularly between rival political leaders, size matters. It is worth remembering Trump's infamous exchange with Marco Rubio – the one that I referred to a couple of chapters ago – because slash writers certainly do. They frequently employ a binary where Trump's small package is explicitly compared to Putin's. With the exception of *Casino in the Kremlin* – the only pro-Trump narrative in my sample – Putin's member is always described as oversized, or "massive" in *Putin the Moves on Trump*.[16] Other writers like to assign more precise measurements; in those stories, Putin's penis is at least ten inches and sometimes a foot long. By contrast, his American lover is given a "baby sized," a "micro," a "one inch," or a "two inch" penis. Moreover, Trump frequently ejaculates prematurely or at inopportune times.

This binarism is important because in romance stories, alpha males always have big penises and their partners have lots of orgasms. As professor Catherine Roach puts it in her book, *Happily Ever After: The Romance Story in Popular Culture*: "Women in romance fiction experience incredible sex. The heroes are masterfully sensitive, skilled, and attentive lovers, with complete control over their sexual response (no erectile dysfunction or premature ejaculation for these men). The heroines enjoy guaranteed orgasms, often through penis-in-vagina intercourse."[17] In other words, sexuality and sexual performance are crucial in constructions of the ideal man. Under those circumstances, making Trump a less-than-ideal lover is a way to attack first his masculinity and next his ability to lead the United States. As Jackson Katz puts it, albeit without extending his analysis to sexual prowess, "every four years, voters decide not only which party best represents their worldviews or interests; they vote for the type of man they want to see as the chief executive, commander in chief, and symbolic head of the nation."[18]

In addition to the focus on size, there seems to be no limit to what slash writers can dream up vis-à-vis Putin's sperm. Their outlandish suggestions take Putin's hyper-masculinity to new heights and add all kinds of satirical elements to the stories. Two narratives incorporate food as an element. The plot of *Pootin on the Tramp* – the story where the two men were college roommates – revolves around that most Russian of food, beets. More specifically, almost every day that they live together, Putin forces Trump to use a beet as a butt plug. This detail may remind some readers that, during the 2016 US election, artist Fernando Sosa made a Trump butt plug to protest the candidate's homophobia. When asked about his work, Sosa said he thinks of it as a 3D political cartoon.[19] Returning to the story, in the evenings, the beet is removed so that Putin can make borscht for his partner to consume. Putin makes sure to ejaculate into the mug first, letting his sperm replace the more traditional sour cream; as he puts it in the story, "I however am sweeter than smetana." Over time, the concoction gives Trump's skin an orange hue that he is forced to duplicate with spray tan once his Russian roommate leaves the university.

The second food reference, made almost in passing, introduces the idea that Putin produces copious amounts of sperm. In *Putin the Moves on Trump*, the Russian president chooses to pull out as he is about to climax, so he ejaculates all over Trump's face and hair. Readers are told that "it was like Trump was smacked in the face with a rather large banana cream pie." Mathias Gannon's *A Strange and Disturbing Love Story* goes even further; there the text says that Putin pushed almost a quart of sperm into his partner's anus and relished every moment of it because, to "Vladimeer Putin, it was like inseminating America itself." The men then spend the next several pages chatting about Putin's super-semen. A backstory, where Putin was subjected to a KGB fertility experiment, is provided to explain how he defies normal biology. The author returns to the subject when he wants to wrap up the narrative. Trump has been discredited at home, and Putin fears that his people will discover that he enjoys the very kind of sex that his government has worked to suppress.[20] So the pair decide to use Putin's entire supply of KGB super-sperm-producing medicine as a way of committing suicide. Putin's almost foot-long penis swells to almost twice its usual size and makes Trump feel like he is being fisted. As Putin climaxes,

Trump's body doubles in size. "The sheer volume of semen being forcefully pumped into him left him speechless and unable to make a sound aside from a few gasps." The men have just enough time to mouth "I love you" to each other before their bodies explode, which brings the story to a close.

Sperm that kills should be a tough act to top, but in the strange world of Putin/Trump slash it is not. Reminiscent of the fairy tale of Rumpelstiltskin, where the miller bragged that his daughter could spin straw into gold, *Pootin on the Tramp* ends with Putin's semen doing something equally fantastic. As the Russian leader ejaculates into Trump's anus, money shoots out of the American's mouth. Then, in *Back-Door Politics*, Putin's erect penis penetrates straight through his partner's pants, uncannily leaving a hole shaped like the onion dome of a Russian Orthodox church. Again, Putin's semen is shown defying biology: when he climaxes, his sperm travels all the way to Trump's stomach, causing the latter to vomit up bits of semen-covered steak. While about as far removed as possible from the morality tales read to children, these stories have a fairy tale quality to them, and the villains do get their comeuppance in the end.

———•———

Bill Clinton's indiscretions with Monica Lewinsky made sex – particularly when it involved public officials in their workplaces – a much more public matter. As the thirteen-month scandal played out in the media, Americans were forced to think about the White House – one of the nation's most sacred spaces and the site of Clinton's most infamous encounter with the intern – in new ways.[21] It is clear that some people were outraged and considered the Oval Office (and the adjacent spaces Clinton actually used with Lewinsky) to have been defiled. George W. Bush, who campaigned on the idea that he would restore honour, dignity, and decency to the White House, brought in a special crew to perform a kind of cleaning exorcism as soon as he was inaugurated.[22] The two dozen cleaners started working four minutes after Bush took the oath of office and ensured that any physical remnants of Clinton's affair were erased.[23] Critics of Clinton used his sexual escapades as a way to critique his policies and his presidency in general. Even if their efforts failed – Clinton's approval ratings actually went up in the year after the affair was revealed – a new measure had been introduced into American political culture, meaning that sexualized discourse could now be weaponized, particularly if it invoked inappropriate behaviour involving symbols of state and/or sacred spaces.[24]

Before launching into a discussion of how Trump/Putin slash does exactly that, it is important to note that the occasional narrative also mocks Russian political symbols and locations. In the works where Trump visits Putin, the Kremlin looms large in the background. The area that encompasses the Kremlin – from its red-brick government buildings and several churches to the vast space of Red Square outside the fortress's walls – is a landscape that is steeped in political power. In imperial times, even after the capital had been moved to St Petersburg, Romanov emperors returned to Moscow and the Kremlin to be crowned. Following the 1917 October Revolution, well-known Soviet leaders were buried in the Kremlin walls, and Lenin's mausoleum, arguably the Soviet Union's most sacred place, was built at their base. Starting in the 1930s and continuing across many decades, Soviet visual propaganda used images of the Kremlin clock tower as a shorthand to refer to state power. So, if anyone wanted to be irreverent about Russian political culture, mocking the Kremlin would be a good place to start.

Two works of slash take a crack at it. In Will Smut's *Putin It in Trump*, the American president gets an erection as his car approaches the Kremlin and he glimpses the clock tower for the first time. Trump is aroused by that most phallic symbol, although the author also takes the time to cut him back down to size, so to speak, by saying it was difficult for anyone to notice his arousal given that Trump's penis was so small. *Casino in the Kremlin* by Gen. Clip "Dingle" Meatus, the earliest piece of Trump/Putin slash, in turn has the US president get turned on as he enters the elevator that will take him to meet his Russian counterpart somewhere in a network of underground bunkers and prison cells underneath the structure. The act of descending into the bowels of the Kremlin complex is, of course, a symbolic penetration of one man by the other, and hints at the power dynamic that shapes the entire invented story. Meatus's work is the only one in our sample that features a dominant Trump besting his rival and lover. Perhaps it is fitting, then, that the novel ends with the real estate developer turned president deciding to turn the Kremlin into a casino, suggesting that Russia's seat of power is somehow fake and certainly no better than a tacky Vegas-style building.

When other Russian symbols of state are invoked in the slash – and admittedly those references are few and far between – they show Putin expressing his patriotism in a sexualized way. In *Casino in the Kremlin*, for instance, Putin sports a red and yellow thong that looks like it has been made from an old Soviet flag. Lester Moorehead's *Putin the Moves on Trump* has even more blatant examples. In a sauna scene when a rather hesitant Trump makes a pass at Putin by touching his penis, the latter "closed his eyes and thought of Russia" before allowing Trump to continue and give him a blow job. The wording may remind readers of a famous English expression that comes from an entry in the 1912 journal of British Lady Hillingdon, describing how she handled the unwanted sexual advances of her husband. While the phrase is sometimes erroneously attributed to Queen Victoria, more generally it refers to the idea that sex is the unwelcome price that women must pay for the economic security they gain from marriage.[25] In this instance, Putin allows the contact with Trump to ensure that he can manipulate the man in the future and secure his country's stance in international relations. Putin is similarly motivated when the pair have sex at the end of the story. As Putin thrusts his penis into the American's anus, he distracts himself by singing the Russian national anthem. In the process, he shows just how devoted he is to his country.

References to the trappings of American political culture are far more prevalent in Trump/Putin slash. Many have a carnivalesque feel to them since they mock or invert things that many Americans hold sacred. Like the pornography that was used to critique the French and Russian monarchs on the eve of their respective revolutions, the stories also suggest that Trump, via his relationship with the Russian president, will denigrate the office he holds, and is consequently not an acceptable leader of the nation. In these instances, the slash pairing holds Putin up as the most extreme foil imaginable for the American leader. For example, *Dolan D. Tramp's Sissy Inauguration* by Aurora Sparks uses the colours of the US flag in a shocking way (although Putin waving a red, white, and blue dildo at Trump in *Excess of Evil: An Alternatively Factual Trump/Putin Romance* is arguably worse). Sparks also undermines the sanctity of inauguration day by constructing a story around the sexual fetish of sissification.[26] In this kind of transvestite porn, a man is forced to cross-dress by an authority figure. The clothing is often described in some detail, because that puts the transgression of gendered cultural norms about dress at the heart of the narrative. Eventually the dress-up sessions lead to sex, but the power dynamics are never reversed, meaning that the person being sissified remains submissive.

In Sparks's story, dominatrix Hillary Clinton arranges for Trump to wear a red, white, and blue sequined dress under his suit during the presidential inauguration, thereby degrading the American flag and a sacred political ritual at the same time. After taking the oath of office, Trump reveals the dress to the crowd before proceeding to go down on his knees to fellate Bill Clinton. The shirtless Russian president then arrives by helicopter, like a television guest star ready to take control of the scene. Putin cuts open the back of Trump's sparkly dress and proceeds to sodomize him. Sparks describes the moment from Trump's perspective: "I arched my back, the better to let Russian president Vladislav Poutine plump the depths of my digestive system. Then I tilted my head back so that Dill Blinton could slide his rock-hard prick into my esophasgus [*sic*]. All of my aspirations, whether political or entrepreneurial, had been forgotten. I wanted nothing more than to act as a passive toy for their pleasure." The wording of that last sentence is significant, going against everything that the American president is supposed to embody. The presidency often operates on a binary system where men are depicted as sexually aggressive warriors, and women only appear as passive figures in need of defending.[27] It is also worth remembering that, as Jackson Katz puts it, "What drew people to Trump was his over-the-top performance of a kind of can-do white masculinity that had been in decline in recent decades."[28] Trump supporters expect their man to be an active, indeed some might say belligerent and aggressive, leader. In other words, they want the exact opposite of the man depicted in *Dolan D. Tramp's Sissy Inauguration*. The story, plausibly in the circumstances, ends with Trump being impeached within twenty-four hours. Putin, whose position as an alpha male was never in question, is angered by this turn of events and proceeds to launch nuclear weapons in response.

Once the real inauguration day came and went without incident, slash writers had to consider how Trump actually governs when he is at work in the Oval Office. His love of signing executive orders, for example, was ridiculed in two of the works in our sample. In *Pootin on the Tramp: Tremendous Erotica, the Best Erotica*, Putin's familiar chiselled muscles so excite the American president that one of the first things he does is sign an executive order deeming Putin the sexiest man in the world. While silly, the moment implies that Trump only wishes to flatter the Russian, as if he has a schoolgirl crush. On the other hand, in *Trump and Putin, A Strange and Disturbing Love Story*, the mention of executive orders is tied to a much more explicit visual: Trump is fantasizing about Putin bending him over the desk in the Oval Office and signing executive orders while he is being sodomized. "The thought of exerting absolute power while being overpowered made Donald Trump hornier than a lonely farmer at a petting zoo," according to the author. The scene is reminiscent of the colouring book that I used to open chapter 3, and it makes whatever Bill Clinton actually did in the same location seem tame by comparison.

The White House occupies a special place in the Trump/Putin narratives. The building appears on the cover of *Back-Door Politics: Volume 1 of the Memoirs of Donald Trump as Told to His Best Friend* (fig. 5.3), and references to the Situation Room, the press briefing room, the Lincoln Bedroom, and of course the Oval Office are scattered across a number of works. The locations serve different purposes depending on the author's overall plot line. For instance, the White House serves only as a minor backdrop in *Mr. Trump Meets Mr. Putin* by Dayn Rand. In this piece of "curtainfic" (a kind of fan fiction centred on domestic activities, named for the notion that its protagonists could believably shop for curtains together),[29] Trump seems to have morphed into Martha Stewart: the president passes his day picking flowers and preparing meals for the staff. After Vladimir Putin parachutes in for a visit – he literally lands on the White House lawn after jumping from a damaged helicopter – Trump cooks him dinner. The remainder of the story, which traces the pair's evolving romantic and political relationship, takes place in other locations, meaning that the White House is not needed as a continual symbol for Rand's political commentary.

The two men's partnership is also indicated at the end of Lester Moorehead's *Putin the Moves on Trump*, when the pair wake up together in the Lincoln Bedroom; in the brief conversation that ensues, they refer to each other as "co-president." According to the White House Museum website, this bedroom is "best known

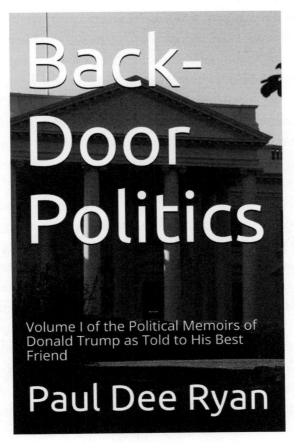

5.3 Screenshot of front cover of
Back-Door Politics.

as a guest room used by presidents to reward friends and political supporters," so by choosing this room rather than any other
bedroom, the author underscores the perceived relationship
between Trump and Putin.[30] He puts Putin in the inner sanctum
of American politics.

However, far different things are implied in *Excess of Evil* and
Back-Door Politics. These two texts use the White House's sacred
spaces as the settings for sexualized episodes and seem to impugn
the morality of all who work in the building as a result. In the first

story, Vice-President Mike Pence masturbates in the Oval Office
with a KKK-style hood placed over his penis. Presidential advisor
Steve Bannon walks in and decides to join the action. Bannon
whips Pence with a riding crop he just happens to be carrying,
before forcing him to perform oral sex on him. Given that both
men are homophobic in real life, the scene portrays them as hyp-
ocrites who do not live by the values they espouse. In the case of
Pence, the telling detail of the hood over his penis also unsubtly
labels him a racist.

A state visit by the Russian president is used to open the plot
of our second example. Such events are special occurrences in
American political life: White House visits by world leaders can,
in the words of professor David Chidester, "be regarded as ritual
pilgrimages to the sacred center of the world."[31] In his account of
the separate visits that Nelson Mandela and F.W. de Klerk made
to the US in 1990, Chidester includes a quotation from a South
African newspaper: "If Washington is the world's informal capital
and the United States president its most powerful man, the Oval
Office in the White House must surely be a very important place."[32]
That is why the text of *Back-Door Politics*, with its conspicuous
lack of veneration or awe for these spaces, is so shocking. The
description of Trump's state dinner for Putin is filled with details
that defile the moment by referencing bodily functions. They
are reminiscent of the way in which *Hustler* magazine – typically
seen as a particularly low-brow publication – treats the body. As
Laura Kipnis observes, "It's insistently material, defiantly vulgar,
corporeal. In fact, the *Hustler* body is often a gaseous, fluid-emit-
ting, embarrassing body, one continually defying the strictures of
social manners and mores and instead governed by its lower intes-
tinal tract."[33] As Kipnis goes on to note, the magazine's humour
is "based on exaggeration and inversion, which have long been
staples of pornographic political satire."[34] I think her words apply
just as well to this piece of slash, given that during the evening

the author has Trump's son Eric urinate into another guest's water glass, while the incontinent president leaves a mess all over the dance floor as he does the tango with "man of steel" Vladimir Putin. The latter remains firmly in control of his body throughout the scene, a stark contrast to the American leader who comes across as totally unsuitable for his position.

———•———

I have argued throughout this chapter that Trump/Putin slash is an important form of political commentary in contemporary America, and needs to be read as such. The works I discussed build upon familiar and well-established aspects of the Russian leader's public image. It is easy to imagine Putin taking charge of dangerous situations in extreme circumstances or in distant locations because that is what people are used to seeing when they watch television, read a newspaper, or go online. Vladimir Putin has been the poster boy for hyper-masculinity since his image makeover of the mid-2000s. As a result, Putin as a fictional character provides the perfect starting point for anyone who wants to use fiction to attack other political figures, notably American leaders who are expected to conform to ideals of masculinity if they are deemed to be successful.

Putin is especially useful when writers wish to impugn US president Donald Trump. The perceived bromance between the two men has inspired a wealth of texts suggesting that the pair enjoy more than mutual admiration. Here, slash writers are tapping into a tradition that goes back hundreds of years, whereby works of pornography were used to undermine the stature and reputation of political leaders. Slash, in this context, is a form of resistance, particularly to people who may be dismayed by the election of the American president. As Bobby put it in his Amazon review of *Mr. Trump Meets Mr. Putin* near the end of the 2016 campaign, "Read what do you think this would be like, do you think it is great?"

"I think it is ██. ██ is power. Right now woman has power," said Vlad. "I know what you want Donald. Shut off movie and shut up."

Donald shut his mouth and shut off the film.

"████████████████ and lean over bed."

████████████████████████████████

██████████████████████████

█████

██████████████████ instructed Vlad.

Donald   acquiesced   and
████████████████████████████████
████████████████████████████████
████████████████████████████████
████████████████████████████████
████████████████████████████████
████████████████████████████████

5.4 Screenshot showing "redacted" page in Chesty LaRou's *Putin on the Trump: Censored Edition*.

this story. You will get a kick in your kindle, a wick for your candle, and a light at the end of this crazy election tunnel."

But that is not all, because most Trump/Putin narratives also imply that the Russians meddled in, and continue to influence, American politics. That is most evident in the new version of Chesty LaRou's *Putin on the Trump*, which was published by Amazon Digital Services LLC on 11 September 2017. In this "censored edition," bits of the story were blacked out as if the pages were part of a top-secret government document (fig. 5.4). References to things like Putin's semen were gone, leaving holes in sentences throughout the story, and the entire final sex scene was covered up. The deliberate and very visible mutilation of the text can lead readers to believe that a political cover-up exists — ensuring that no one will ever know the full extent of the relationship between the two presidents. Reviewers of other works express similar ideas. The most forceful is Claire McGuire, who had this to say in her comments about *Trump and Putin, A Strange and Disturbing Love Story*: "The points made are unfortunately true ... Putins [sic] control of the Trump election and plans to resurrect the USSR are no joke. Getting the Trump voters to accept this will not happen until their own asses are directly affected. The majority of US voters who voted against Trump have realize [sic] how Putin controls their future, livelihoods and very lives!"[35]

McGuire's view of Putin as an arch-villain and evil mastermind fits well with Putin's image in the globalized public sphere. Since we have already seen how that notion has been expressed through material culture and different kinds of unmediated fiction, all that remains is to explore Putin's digital presence.

6

Putin at Your Fingertips
The Online Presence of the Russian President

My favourite piece of Putin kitsch is a fake toy. What I mean is that the actual item – a Putin action figure – was never made, but the idea, and more importantly an image of what the toy would have looked like, lives on in cyberspace. Someone named Chris Barker came up with it. He actually created a whole "21st Century Bastards" series of fake toys devoted to world leaders and public figures he does not like.[1] David Cameron, Nigel Farage, and Piers Morgan, for example, are joined by Steve Bannon, Sean Spicer, Kellyanne Conway, and of course Donald Trump. All are amusing, but my absolute favorite is "Action Vlad." As you can see from the picture, the packaging suggests that he would have come with a "complete world domination kit," with a machine gun and "pee pee tape," as well as "adjustable limbs and morals" (fig. 6.1). As per usual, Putin wears only a pair of combat pants, leaving his impressive pectoral muscles bare, and he is ready for action. Well, he would be if he was real. Like everything else we will discuss in this chapter, "Action Vlad" lacks material form,

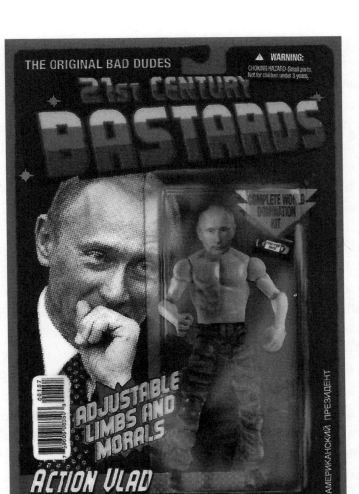

6.1 "Action Vlad," the action figure that
never was, printed onto a fridge magnet.

but via the internet can still influence our impressions of the
Russian leader.

This chapter focuses on what I call "Virtual Putin." In other words,
I look at the way in which the Russian president's image pervades the
digital world and how it has been played with in things like memes

and parodies as well as apps and video games. Readers will see, at the end of the chapter, that I even checked into Putin's presence in online porn. It is important to address these subjects because, as one internet scholar put it, "We use social media in the service of sharing values as a way of communicating our experience of the world and bonding with others."[2] In other words, the ways in which people refer to, manipulate, and share the image of the Russian leader can reflect their political values, as well as their need to reach out to like-minded individuals. The rise of Web 2.0 – whereby the internet has changed from being a giant version of *Encyclopedia Britannica* to a multidirectional resource that facilitates communication between people – makes that possible.

Now, I must admit before we delve into the Putin material that it is difficult to truly judge the intentions of people who develop, post, play with, and comment on digital kitsch. Moreover, trolls abound in cyberspace, and given the charges that they have interfered in several Western elections, they clearly take an interest in politics.[3] The problem is that it is hard to tell the difference between the postings of a troll and those of an opinionated or politically engaged person. That dilemma is spelled out in something that media scholars Whitney Phillips and Ryan Milner refer to "Poe's Law." It suggests that "sincere extremism online (manifesting as bigotry, conspiracy theorizing, or simply being wrong about something) is often indistinguishable from satirical extremism."[4] Unfortunately, much digital kitsch can be read both ways, so we may not be able to tell the difference with 100 per cent accuracy. With that said, we cannot throw up our hands in despair or simply ignore what is out there, either. The digital manifestations of Putin's celebrity are too widespread, and arguably too important, for that. Instead, to quote a popular meme, we will "keep calm and carry on," all the while knowing that with flawed sources you cannot guarantee definitive conclusions.

—·—

The outcome of the 2006 US midterm elections was decided – at least in part – by a video uploaded to YouTube, a website that had only been around for a year.[5] The now infamous incident, where the Republican incumbent senator for Virginia George Allen referred to his opponent's staffer using the racial slur "macaca," was uploaded to YouTube almost immediately and then viewed by several million people. Allen not only lost his Senate seat, thereby swinging control of that body to the Democrats, but he also lost any chance of ever running for the White House.[6] Nor were his fortunes the only ones affected by videos on YouTube in that election cycle. Senator Conrad Burns (R-Montana) got into trouble for racist remarks, and unflattering clips of senators Joseph Lieberman (D-Connecticut) and Jim Talent (R-Missouri) were similarly uploaded to the site.[7]

The flip side of the YouTube coin, where candidates can sometimes harness or ride a wave of positive press, is perhaps best exemplified by the popular reaction to Barack Obama's "Yes We Can" speech. Obama's words inspired some supporters to create mashups and post them on the web. The most well known was done by will.i.am of the Black-Eyed Peas; in only a few weeks, the video he uploaded to YouTube had been watched more than 13 million times. In other words, it had five times more views than a presidential debate hosted by CNN.[8] The official Obama campaign did equally well when it came to reaching young people via digital technology. In addition to its blogging communities and its use of Twitter and email to message followers, the campaign launched the YouTube channel "BarackObamadotcom," which garnered 20 million views.[9]

These two sets of examples reveal the yin and yang nature of the internet, a technology that occupies an increasingly important position in American political life. Admittedly, not everyone has guaranteed access to a computer or the skills needed to create a digital text, but most people can at least view a video, comment on a social media post, or share a meme – all behaviours that reinforce the horizontal nature of current political conversations. However mundane, the activities are significant, as scholars of digital media use in authoritarian nations are quick to point out.[10] In all contexts, however, humour is often the key, because it both attracts attention and can act as a form of resistance when it is wielded against political elites. That is why so many internet memes and YouTube videos are funny. Indeed, the familiar phrasal templates used in most memes automatically set them up as jokes. For example, the "In Soviet Russia ... sexy isn't back ... it was never authorized to leave" meme, which features a muscled Putin giving a Mona Lisa–like smile for the camera, is a typical "Russian reversal meme" (fig. 6.2). That type of joke may originate with 1980s comedian Yakov Smirnoff, who used to compare life in America and the USSR in his stand-up routines.[11] Here, though, the image plays with the sexualized masculinity of Vladimir Putin to make a point about the authoritarian nature of the Russian political system.

As we have seen throughout this book, that meme is not an isolated example. Indeed, so many moments from Putin's career lend themselves to memes. Some, like the invasion of Ukraine, are serious, while others, like the Russian leader putting on a pair of sunglasses, are not. Putin's physical appearance has been commented upon extensively. In just the images gathered in *Best Putin Memes: Funniest Memes*, his face is compared to that of a dog, several cats, Dobby the House Elf (from the *Harry Potter* films), and Dr Evil, the villain in the *Austin Powers* movies.[12] Other examples merge his likeness with that of Eminem or Justin Bieber. Finally, Vladimir Putin's name lends itself perfectly to all sorts of jokes. "Putin" can become "poutine" (the Canadian dish of French fries and cheese curds smothered in gravy), as well as the verb "putting." The best play on "Vladimir" has to be a meme that marked the stages of Putin's life: a photograph of him as a child was labelled "Ladimir," then he became "Dadimir" in a picture with his wife and an infant

In Soviet Russia...

Sexy isn't back...

it was never authorized to leave

6.2 "In Soviet Russia ... sexy isn't back ...
it was never authorized to leave" meme.

daughter. Other photographs captured President Putin in a variety of emotional states: Putin with tears on his cheeks became "Sadimir," an angry Putin giving a speech was "Madimir," and Putin caught laughing was "Gladimir." Separate memes that show Putin skateboarding play with the moniker "Radimir." I could go on and on, but it is perhaps more constructive to just use one case study and analyze its permutations to get a sense of a meme's circulation across the internet and the playfulness of its manifestations.

In May 2010, the Huffington Post named "Putin on the Ritz" the #1 Worst Visual Pun of All Time.[13] Obviously, that endorsement, and the fact that almost a decade later the meme is still around, makes it the perfect example for discussing the lifespan and evolution of a Putin meme. The song "Putting on the Ritz" was originally published by Irving Berlin in December 1929; its title came from a slang expression for dressing fashionably when going out. The tune is best remembered for the song and dance version performed by Fred Astaire in the film *Blue Skies* (1946), although countless other singers have recorded it before and since.[14] The image shown here, for instance, clearly references the film, but casts Putin in the iconic role instead of Astaire (fig. 6.3).

The enduring quality of the association is apparent in our next example, figure 6.4. The image shows the Russian president in the kind of top hat needed to do the dance routine, and it says that the "Putin on the Ritz World Tour" will take place in 2017 – in other words, a full seven years after the Huffington Post originally slammed the meme.

Apart from these static images, the "Putin on the Ritz" meme has sparked actual song and dance interpretations that have been uploaded to YouTube and other internet sites. These include a music video where the heads of Vladimir Putin and George W. Bush have been superimposed onto people dancing in a Hollywood-style musical. That one was put on YouTube in May 2008 and has only 576,087 views, despite the fact that its quality is much better than many other Putin memes.[15] More people will remember a video that was uploaded to YouTube by persons unknown in March 2012, right on the eve of the Russian presidential election that year. Within only a couple of weeks, almost three million people had watched the footage that shows a flash mob dancing to Berlin's tune on Moscow's Sparrow Hills. The mystery surrounding the

6.3 "Putin on the Ritz" with Putin as Fred Astaire.

6.4 "Putin on the Ritz World Tour 2017."

flash mob's organization, as well as how the file wound up on the internet, allowed people to speculate that Putin's own political party, United Russia, may have been behind the incident, since it had arranged earlier flash mobs to offer support for its leader during the campaign.[16] Or the act could just as easily have been an anti-Putin protest. The point is that no one was sure. But everyone was talking about it, and occasionally emulating the moment. One blogger based in Vladivostok, for instance, captured video footage of young people in a local dance studio doing their own version at a recital. "I was grinning like a fool by the time they were done, for the humorous song choice and for how much fun the students were clearly having," she wrote in her 12 April 2012 post.[17]

In time, the meme evolved as people decide to play with the word "ritz" as well. One example comments on Putin's divorce by captioning a photograph of the Russian leader and his former spouse with the words "Putin on the Quits." But by far the most prevalent association is with the brand of crackers that Nabisco introduced back in 1934. The internet is frankly awash in manipulated pictures of Putin's face superimposed on a Ritz cracker (fig. 6.5), him standing or sitting on a box of the snacks (fig. 6.6), and so on. One variant even has Putin in a traditional Russian folk costume standing on a box of the crackers in front of the Kremlin wall. Other images fall back on references to Putin's physique by depicting him as a heavily muscled bodybuilder on a cracker, or as a cave man standing on a crushed one (fig. 6.7). Finally, some enterprising soul replaced the horse in one of Putin's vacation photographs with the iconic cracker (fig. 6.8). This particular meme has been circulating both as a static image and as an animated GIF since at least 2012. My favourite of the animations even features Fred Astaire singing "Putting on the Ritz" in the background while Putin rides on and on.[18]

Since I wanted to reproduce them as illustrations, I ordered copies of the memes that I have just been talking about from

6.5   Putin on Ritz crackers.

6.6   Putin and Ritz cracker boxes.

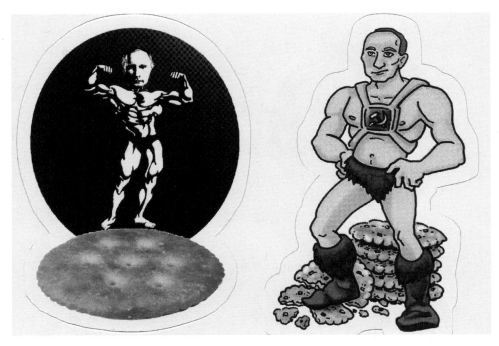

6.7   Muscled Putin on the Ritz.

Redbubble.com – a print-on-demand service based in Australia but with offices in San Francisco and Berlin. I was also hoping that this might help me learn something about who might be engaging with the meme, at least enough to want to profit from it. According to the information in Redbubble's profiles (admittedly not a perfect source), I found that the designers were dispersed across the globe. A majority – six out of ten – said they lived in the United States, while two were listed as residing in the UK and another was in Australia. The final person chose not to reveal his location in his profile. Only one designer was female. Perhaps most surprisingly, I found few signs of widespread political engagement as I perused the other images that the same people had available in their storefronts. "JonFun1" appeared to be the most politically driven of the bunch, with listings featuring memes of Lenin, Theresa May, and

6.8   Putin riding a Ritz cracker.

a reworking of *American Gothic* that superimposed Donald and Melania Trump onto the original, but the majority of his designs touched on everyday subjects rather than politics. "MoStorm Trooper," on the other hand, apparently loves memes about the US television program *The Office* since they dominate his offerings, and "spinningvisions" produces designs about bowling, dogs, and fishing. In the end, I was left wondering about the banality of the Putin on the Ritz meme because, although I think its various permutations show how deeply ingrained images of the Russian president have become in popular consciousness, I got no sense that most of them were created for political reasons.

That is obviously not the case with our final example, however. The Putin on the Ritz meme came full circle, so to speak, in 2017. That is because in February American comedian Randy Rainbow uploaded a new video to YouTube and his personal website. Rainbow is known for his politicized parodies of musical numbers, which means that his interpretation of the meme went from playful to packing quite a political punch. In his "Putin and the Ritz" video, he artfully combined the song and dance genre with the Ritz cracker reference by transforming Donald Trump, a man famous for his use of spray tan and resultant orange-hued skin, into the cracker.[19] His tongue-in-cheek suggestions that the men share a sexual relationship are much tamer than some of the more flagrant items discussed in this book, but they are still a notable feature of the parody. Despite the current debate over whether such materials – meaning anything that sexualizes the relationship between the two men – are homophobic, the video has garnered very positive reviews from the LGBTQ community.[20] It has also been viewed more than 350,000 times on YouTube alone.

Kremlin officials seldom acknowledge the ways in which Putin's name and image have been reworked in memes and YouTube parodies like the ones that I have analyzed here. However, that does not mean that those things pass by the watchful eyes of the Russian authorities unnoticed. Roskomnadzor (the federal censorship agency of the Russian government) did remind Russian social media users in 2015 that it was illegal to use "a photo of a public figure to embody a popular internet meme which has nothing to do with the celebrity's personality." People who violate the law can be asked to remove their memes and parodies or face lawsuits for defamation, but none of the cases that have proceeded so far have involved the president's likeness.[21] Apart from garnering international headlines, Roskomnadzor's statement seems to have had little effect on the proliferation of Putin memes. Instead, more and more of them flood into cyberspace every day, as people around the world look to this form of digital technology to express their senses of humour and perhaps their political opinions.

———•———

Like millions of others, when I get bored waiting for my food in restaurants or in line at the bank, I turn to my phone to pass the time. For months, my go-to app has been *Putin Moscow Crazy Style*, which lets me give the Russian president a makeover and then pose him against a variety of backgrounds (fig. 6.9). I find it hilarious that I can make Putin appear so ridiculous, and get a subversive thrill from knowing that I could also post my images on Facebook if I so desired. *Putin Moscow Crazy Style*, which is really just a kind of digital colouring book, was created by Irina Vragova and has been available for both iPhones and Android devices since February 2017. More than 5,000 people have downloaded this particular app, although that figure pales in comparison with the estimated 500,000 people who may have played something similar: the *Putin Gay Dress-Up* video game.[22] That was released during the Sochi Olympics as a sign of support for Russia's embattled LGBTQ community, which had seen its legal rights severely curtailed the year before. While the game is no longer available, an article about it lists some of the sexually explicit accessories the developer included in Putin's potential wardrobe – everything from strap-on dildos to Pussy Riot T-shirts to drag outfits.[23] As is the case with my much tamer game, the final images could be shared with friends via Facebook. Like the colouring books that have appeared periodically throughout this book, both *Putin Gay Dress-Up* and *Putin Moscow Crazy Style* are pieces of kitsch; they just happen to be digital rather than material objects.

I do not think this kind of game was what scholars had in mind when they began to address whether gaming – broadly

6.9 *Putin Moscow Crazy Style* sample creation.

defined – could have an impact on the civic engagement of young people. Ten years ago, the Pew Internet and American Life Project, with support from the MacArthur Foundation, surveyed just over 1,100 teenagers (and their parents) about video gaming habits. The researchers behind the survey were keenly interested in figuring out if there was a connection between video game playing and civics. They found that gaming was nearly universal behaviour for this cohort, with 97 per cent of the teens doing it.[24] But the results concerning the impact of all that gaming were less conclusive. According to the final report, "Neither the frequency of game play nor the amount of time young people spend playing games is significantly related to most of the civic and political outcomes that we examined – following politics, persuading others how to vote, contributing to charities, volunteering, or staying informed about politics and current events." In the end, no one could definitively say that gaming either undermined or encouraged civic participation.

There is no evidence to suggest that the percentage of people who play video games has declined since that Pew survey, and the jury is ultimately still out on whether gaming can lead to greater civic awareness or more participatory political behaviour.[25] But we can say for certain that a wider array of games is available than ever before, and their creation may signal that developers, at least, are combining their desire for income with political messages. The growing number of games is a result of the introduction of smartphones. The iPhone premiered at the Worldwide Developers Conference in June 2007 and, at that time, a mere eleven apps had been developed. They were the rather boring things – like the calendar and address book – that come standard in all phones today. But the potential for more apps was readily apparent, so their number grew at a rather astonishing rate. By March 2008, the number of apps had seen a hundredfold increase, and that was before Apple launched a software development kit

(SDK) that would allow third-party developers to make apps for its devices. Steve Jobs was able to proudly announce in his keynote address at the next developers conference that the SDK had been downloaded a quarter of a million times in the first three months after it was released. At the same time, 25,000 people had registered as developers with Apple in this way.[26]

The iPhone changed the nature of video gaming because it put a gaming platform into the hands of every smartphone owner, even ones who refuse to own a PlayStation or Xbox. My colleague at Concordia University, Dr Mia Consalvo, notes that as a result, "the iPhone began transforming smartphones into agents of play." She means "play" broadly defined "to include not only games but also nonserious applications such as ring tones, screen savers, horoscopes, and sports applications."[27] Once people's creativity was unleashed, the number of apps grew astronomically. By 2011, more than 15 billion apps had been downloaded to Apple devices, and the company's App Store housed over half a million to choose from.[28] Not to be outdone, tech giant Google quickly followed Apple's example; it too released a software development kit available for people interested in making apps for Android devices.

On the surface, this gaming revolution appears to have many of the hallmarks of participatory culture. Developers from across the globe are involved, and they do not need to be employed by large corporations. Similar to the print-on-demand companies that made possible all that Putin kitsch from chapters 2 and 3, companies like Apple, Google, and Amazon act as hosts for more localized initiatives. They do maintain some oversight of the contents of apps. Apple, for instance, vets apps according to its own interpretation of "appropriateness," as well as to make sure they meet certain technical standards.[29] But far more control over content really lies in the hands of the developers, since it is they who set the parameters for what is possible in each game. As Howard Gardner and Katie Davis put it in their book, *The App Generation*, "As a result of a programmer's (often arbitrary) design decisions, certain actions are possible – indeed encouraged – while others don't even present themselves as options."[30] I understand their point when I think about the options in *Putin Moscow Crazy Style*. If I want to put Putin in a dress, for example, there is only one design available and it only comes in three colours. Arbitrariness is particularly evident when it comes to accessories. I have no idea what a guitar, fairy wand, balloon dog, or hermit crab have to do with the Russian leader, but in this game you can have him carry all of them (but not at the same time, alas). Despite these obvious limitations, I still have an illusion of power when it comes to the app. I chose to put it on my phone and I can delete it if I want to. And it allows me to carry a small virtual Putin with me wherever I go.

The Russian president has proven to be a popular subject in the online marketplace I have been describing. During an interview about his work on a Putin zombie slaying game, Belgian app developer Michele Rocco Smeets explained why he picked the Russian leader to star in it: "Putin has this tough guy image and he's not afraid to get his hands dirty," he said. "He hunts, he rides, he shoots. A leader should be strong, and in my opinion Putin is the only world leader who really fulfils this image."[31] In other words, just as in fan fiction where his image aligned nicely with the qualities typically given to men in romance narratives, Putin's public persona fits what people expect from game heroes. That is why we can find him saving the world from aliens, or fixing his country's economy by collecting gold rubles while also defeating members of the mafia. (Those are the premises of *Putin vs Aliens* and *Putin Saves Russia*, respectively.) Sometimes Putin is pitted against other world leaders. For instance, his rather tense relationship with former US president Barack Obama served as fodder for both *Obama vs Putin* and *Putin vs Obama 2015*. As soon as Obama was replaced by Donald Trump, developers listed new apps such as *Trump vs Putin: Soundboard* and *Mahjong: Putin and Trump Game* in Google

Play. First-person narratives, either tracing Putin's rise to power or following the "day-in-the-life-of-Putin" approach, are among the most popular to feature the Russian president. *Rise of Putin*, for instance, has been installed on more than 10,000 Android devices, and *President 2017* has been installed on more than 100,000, despite the fact that it has gotten some rather poor reviews. And this is just a small sampling of what is out there. If you want Putin to give you answers like a magic eight ball, there's an app for that. If you want a dancing Putin to appear at random moments on your screen, there's an app for that. And if you want a shirtless Putin to jump over things like Mario or Luigi, there's an app for that too.

To be thorough, in mid-July 2018, I also checked what Putin items were available through Steam, a digital distribution platform for video games. Steam is reminiscent of a print-on-demand service (but for video games) because the platform lets independent game developers sell their products through its website, which they do in large numbers. An average of 180 new games are launched on Steam every week.[32] Steam was created by the Valve Corporation in 2003 and has been enormously successful. Two years ago, users purchased more than $4 billion worth of games through Steam, which meant that it garnered just under 20 per cent of the global PC games sales. At the start of this year, the service had more than 150 million registered accounts.[33] Most of them were created by users in North America and Western Europe, although apparently the number of people from China who are on the platform is growing rapidly.

The degree of oversight from Valve varies. When Steam was smaller, staffers personally checked every game to make sure that it worked and that it was not offensive. More recently, Steam has been under fire because Valve has been allowing developers to launch games without vetting them first. Interestingly, the developer singled out for creating homophobic games was St Petersburg–based Nikita "Ghost_Rus," who is also behind roughly one third of the

6.10   *Putinoids vs Navalnyats* video game.

dozen or so Putin games on Steam.[34] According to the Crappy Games Wiki, whose entry on him lists nine reasons why his creations suck, Nikita "Ghost_Rus" started putting his games on Steam in October 2017 and released thirty-six games (not all of them about Putin) in an eight-month period.[35] Puzzlingly, there was some suggestion that his account on Steam was terminated in June 2018 (I was able to see his developer page one week but not the next); however, as of August 2018, all of his materials were back on the site.

And they do suck. The graphics are simplistic and the premises silly. In *Putin vs ISIS*, for instance, Putin is supposed to be saving Syria from terrorists. The Russian leader's face has been superimposed onto a plane that bombs people and trucks on the ground. *Putin Run Away from Trump* has Putin doing nothing more than running away from the American president and his clones while collecting bitcoins. More far-fetched is *Putinoids vs Navalnyats*, a game where two kinds of cyborgs (representing the two different Russian political leaders) shoot water pistols at each other in a bath house (fig. 6.10). According to Steamspy – the

6.11 *Kicking Kittens: Putin Saves the World* video game.

part of the website that tracks the number of people who have bought each game and how long the average user spent playing it – none of the offerings by Nikita "Ghost_Rus" have sold well enough to transcend the lowest category (0–20,000 purchases), and people do not play them for long. The average player of *Putin vs ISIS* lasted just forty-five seconds before clicking on to something else.

To be fair, most of the other Putin games on Steam are just as bad, with stats and playing times to match. They each play with aspects of Putin's public persona that will be familiar to gamers, even the ones who are not particularly interested in politics. For example, in *Kicking Kittens: Putin Saves the World*, the shirtless Russian leader is scored on manliness as he battles to save the planet from aliens who are invading with robots disguised as kittens (fig. 6.11). Once a player has collected all ten symbols of manliness, their Putin avatar can unlock the "Aura of Manliness" and destroy the alien spaceships. I doubt many people got that far since the average playing time of users was just over three minutes. Another game, *Putin, Boobs and Trump*, has Putin fighting to regain power after supposedly losing the 2018 elections. He is shown shooting other world leaders in front of the Lenin mausoleum in Moscow. Even with a warning for nudity, which one might think would attract more buyers, the game is still in the bottom category, and average players spent just under two minutes with it. The most professional-looking game, *Navalny 20!8: The Rise of Evil*, traces the political career of one of Putin's most high-profile political opponents, and is the only one I found that casts Putin as the bad guy (fig. 6.12). Players assume the role of volunteers for the Navalny election campaign and their goal is to collect the 300,000 signatures needed for the candidate to get on the ballot, so that he can hopefully defeat Putin. Despite the fact that the graphics are comparatively good, the game has not sold well (the usual 0–20,000 purchases category), and the average play time is just over thirty seconds. I suspect this last game is really the only one in my sample that is actually designed as a political statement since its backstory requires more political knowledge than the others.

I must be honest. There is no evidence that any of these games are widely played and media attention to them has been pretty sparse. That could be because, in the end, people are not particularly interested in combining gaming and politics. One of my sons suggested something else, however. He argued that the problem actually has more to do with price. Apparently, many Steam users assume games costing less than $1 will be bad, so they stay away from them on principle, playing only games that cost approximately the same thing they would in a brick-and-mortar retail setting. Or if they do purchase bargain games, they give them only a few seconds to keep their attention, arguing that since they have not made a significant financial investment to obtain the game, they do not really lose anything important if they abandon it almost immediately. If my son's theory is correct, game developers who opt to set low prices for their wares may not even realize that they are limiting their potential market right

6.12   *Navalny 20!8: The Rise of Evil* video game.

from the start. Finally, it could be that the subject simply has not yet caught fire. I mean, I never thought the sexualized items that I have spent the past two years working with would find their way into the cultural mainstream, but they have. Maybe the Putin-inspired apps and video games will be the next big thing?

———•———

Given how much space has been devoted in this book to things that are sexually explicit, I thought it only fitting to end by exploring Putin's presence in the world of online porn. The rise of Web 2.0 in the first decade of the new millennium not only changed the landscape of politics by introducing print-on-demand services and spaces for fan fiction to flourish, but it also led to the emergence of Porn 2.0. The term refers to a real revolution in how sexually explicit works are created and circulate.[36] The introduction of new technologies, such as digital cameras and smartphones with cameras, allowed for amateur creations to proliferate and an array of fetishes to become more visible than they had been in the past. The most popular outlet for amateur productions was "tubes" – in other words, websites like YouPorn, Porno Tube, and XTube that were influenced by the enormous popularity of YouTube. To garner a sense of how quickly xxx-rated sites caught on, one need only look at YouPorn. The site was launched in 2006 and had 15 million users within nine months.[37] By June 2008, its Alexa (internet traffic) rank was an impressive 35.[38]

To trace Putin's footprint in this world, I began with the site that has eclipsed all the others: PornHub. PornHub is currently the largest and arguably most influential pornography site on the internet – its Alexa rank was 27 in July 2018.[39] PornHub launched in May 2007 and has offices in various US cities and London, although it remains headquartered in Montreal, the city where I work. The site is navigable in a number of European languages including Russian, although it has run afoul of Roskomnadzor on a couple of occasions, which means that within Russia the site is hard to access.[40] Keeping things simple, I typed "Putin PornHub" into Google. I expected to find loads of parody porn and maybe even a lingering deep fake or two, despite the fact that the latter have been banned on sites like Gfycat, Reddit, and PornHub.[41] The subject headings that came up were promising, but once I clicked on them, I drew a blank.

It turns out that PornHub has no Putin porn on it. Instead, there are two videos that show Putin playing the piano, while another has him making a speech in English. Even less titillating are the videos that show the Russian leader shaking hands with a robot prototype or getting caught in a heavy rainstorm during an official ceremony. Maybe a viewer, at a stretch, might find the 1:58 montage from one of Putin's Siberian vacations sexy, but it recycles footage that can be found in the mainstream media and reveals nothing beyond Putin's ubiquitous naked chest. Putin even remains clothed in a video entitled "Putin's Striptease"; according to the site's metrics, that file has been viewed 4,806 times and 64 per cent of people who rated it gave the video a thumbs up. I am not sure why, because nothing happens. For four minutes, you watch a loop of an animated Putin figure dance in a tuxedo. That's it. A whiff of something sexual appears in the title "Saggy Bottom White Boy Gets Topped by Russian Top," but it turns out that someone is really making a political statement, because the file that was uploaded to Pornhub with that descriptor was actually CNN footage of the entire Putin-Trump press conference after the two men's meeting in Helsinki in July 2018. The label is reminiscent of many of the materials we have already considered in that it invokes sexual positioning to make its point about political power, but no alterations to the actual film were made to increase its sexual content. This case is reminiscent of an incident from four years earlier when the porn site had to intervene and ask its users to stop posting videos that had nothing to do with sex. In that instance, German soccer fans had flooded PornHub with videos from Germany's 7–1 defeat of Brazil, using the title "Young Brazilians get fucked by the entire German Soccer Team" to underscore the magnitude of Brazil's defeat.[42]

I had slightly better luck in the parody department because two very funny Putin parodies have been uploaded to PornHub: "Love the Way You Move" by Slightly Left of Centre, and "Putin, Putout," created by Slovak comedian Klemen Slakonja. Both videos can also be found on YouTube, however, so neither can be considered porn. In the end, the only true pieces of parody porn that I found were on a different site (www.pornfoxvr.com) and both came from what had to be the same one-day shoot. Posted on 21 February 2017, "Vladimir 'the Impaler' Putin Nails Melania" and the longer "Donald Cuckold Trump" feature Angel Wicky and two unnamed men. The one cast as Trump wears a suit most of the time, as well as a truly awful wig. The actor playing Putin is unsurprisingly dressed for a holiday in Siberia, wearing camouflage pants and no shirt. The films share a common descriptor: "The sex tape everyone is talking about! In this gorgeous VR scene we see Putin giving it to Melania while Trump is cuckolded in the corner watching." Actually that is not true of both films – only the first shows our fake Trump tied up in the corner watching the actress playing his wife have sex with the fake Russian president. In the second film, the Trump character has sex with Melania (giving Angel Wicky the best line in either video: "That's how I like America inside me") while she also fellates the actor playing Putin. The action does not drag on long – 1:05 and 5:00 minutes respectively – and the satire packs little punch.

What does it mean that there is so little Putin porn on xxx-rated websites? I suspect it has to do with the divergent goals of the sites and the materials that we have already examined. Porn sites contain images and videos that are intended to turn people on. Pornographied kitsch, on the other hand, is not meant to evoke such sensations, but to get people thinking about politics. Moreover, the pornographication of mainstream American political culture has extended so far that references to explicit sexuality are now part of everyday life, something that causes porn to lose some of its taboo nature. To put it another way, why would anyone need to go to PornHub for political commentary when they can add *Putin F*cks Trump: An Adult Coloring Book for Patriots*, or a T-shirt with a homoerotic design featuring the two presidents, to their Amazon.com grocery order?

———•———

"Thus a more playful style of activism is emerging through this appropriative and transformative dimension of participatory culture."[43] These words by professor Henry Jenkins – a person who has been at the forefront of research into popular and participatory culture for decades – are full of hope. I want to believe them as well. I want to think that all the people who are designing Putin memes and parodies, or who are developing video games about the Russian president, are doing so because they care deeply about politics and the world around them. The changing nature of the internet makes that a distinct possibility, but at the same time, Poe's Law reminds us that ultimately one can never be 100 per cent certain about what drives anyone's online behaviour. Moreover, the evidence from this chapter has been mixed. Clearly, people derive some satisfaction from Putin memes, or those would have disappeared years ago. After all, most memes represent fads, so their lifespans are short. The fact that the "Putin on the Ritz" meme, for instance, is still mutating and circulating after ten years must tell us something, but exactly what remains open for discussion. The same ambiguity pervades my analysis of Putin apps and video games. I know they exist, can describe their contents, and can refer to the information provided by the developers on their pages – but in the end I have no definitive conclusions to offer about their *raison d'etre* or why anyone would play them or not. Ironically, it is only when we come to Putin and his absence from porn websites that the ground becomes less shaky beneath my feet. There, I think my findings support what I have said all along: when Putin's image is pornographied, it is for political reasons and not because anyone truly finds him sexy.

Conclusion

Move Over Elvis,
Putin Is Everywhere

Monday, 16 July 2018, was a surreal kind of day. Russian president Vladimir Putin had a two-hour private meeting with his American counterpart Donald Trump as part of a summit in Helsinki, Finland. The day was capped off by a joint press conference that most US commentators viewed as a disaster for their president. *Time* magazine responded to the event by releasing the cover of its next issue early. The composite image blurred the two men's faces together, making them appear as if they were one person. Nancy Burson, the artist who created the picture, said she wanted to make people "stop and think."[1] By all accounts, the continued warmth that Trump displayed towards Putin that day was puzzling, and led to all kinds of media speculation about the real nature of their relationship. While pundits pondered and sometimes railed about Trump's performance, ordinary people flooded the internet with memes. One that a friend posted to my Facebook wall had Putin leading Trump into the press conference on a leash – when I clicked on it, the data at the bottom said the image had evoked 43K responses (likes, loves, and smiley faces) and had been shared more than 17,000 times.

In New York City on the same day, a man named Jeff Jetton decorated the famous statue of a bull that sits in the middle of Wall Street with 130 dildos before he climbed on its back while wearing a mask of Vladimir Putin. To some commentators, his display was a protest about the perceived role of the Russian in American politics. Jetton himself said that people were free to interpret the scene however they wished, but that he would not disagree with that interpretation. As he later told the Huffington Post, "Anybody who tells you sex toys aren't good tools of resistance has never had a bag of dicks and a little bit of ingenuity."[2]

Meanwhile, the internet was also aflutter over an animated cartoon published to mark the Trump-Putin summit by that bastion of respectable journalism, the *New York Times*. With snippets from speeches and interviews where Trump had spoken positively about Putin playing in the background, the animation sequence depicts the two men on a date that culminates with them making out while riding a unicorn. Many people who saw the cartoon labelled it homophobic, although the newspaper said in an official statement that it was not meant to be viewed that way. "The filmmaker's vision," according to the statement, "was one of teenage infatuation portrayed through a dream-like fantasy sequence. He [the filmmaker] would have used the same format to satirize Trump's infatuation with another politician, regardless of sexuality or gender."[3]

Within two days, a new piece of Trump/Putin slash was uploaded for sale on Amazon.com as well. Two-thirds of the action in *Divided Loyalties: From Russia with Love* was set in a hotel room in Helsinki. Told from the perspective of the American president, the story abounds with the usual superlative-laced monologues one expects from Trump. One of them reveals that he has to agreed to surrender his "anal virginity to a Russian oligarch in exchange for power," which he proceeds to do over the next few pages. In another moment, the president's inner dialogue connects the ability to rule a country with penis size. He sums up that particular thought with two short sentences that underscore much of what I have said above about the construction of presidential masculinity in the United States: "Also, it's why my opponent lost the race," muses fake Trump. "Dicks are a prerequisite for power." In a final act of domination, Vladimir Putin urinates on the man whom the story insists he put into office.

That week, in other words, it suddenly felt like the mainstream media was catching on to everything I have been saying in this book.

Just as a good recipe needs a list of ingredients for it to work, a particular confluence of things and events has led us to this point. First, politics had to become personalized to the point where public officials are now regularly treated as celebrities, and their scandals drive the news cycle. Next, a resurgent Russia became less tentative on the world stage in the first decade of the new millennium. Vladimir Putin has been willing to be typecast as an alpha male and has engaged in a host of media stunts to cement that image in people's minds. New technologies driven by the internet (especially Web 2.0) have democratized the production of political kitsch. Print-on-demand services have led to a flourishing of material kitsch bearing Putin's likeness. Avenues for self-publishing have contributed to that outpouring as well, but they have proven to be just as instrumental in the rise of politicized fan fiction. Finally, the internet is also home to kitsch that lacks any kind of material form – memes, parodies, apps, and video games. Taken together, this deluge reveals that many people have rejected top-down political and media models in favour of something more horizontal and participatory. They have created a truly globalized public sphere, although it must be said that parts of it – the aspects that are heavily sexualized – may offend some who come into contact with it.

Towards the end of this project, I contemplated how the immersion in Putin kitsch has changed me. I thought about another destabilizing moment when people felt like they had fallen down the metaphorical rabbit hole: the destalinization campaigns that followed the death of Soviet leader Joseph Stalin. One of the key works of that time, Alexander Solzhenitsyn's *One Day in the Life of Ivan Denisovich*, which did so much to publicize the conditions in Stalin's gulag, ends with its hero musing about the successes of his day as he lies down to sleep. "Nothing had spoiled the day and it had been almost happy," Ivan concludes. But the final words belong to the omniscient author. Solzhenitsyn reminds readers that "there were three thousand six hundred and fifty-three days like this in his sentence, from reveille to lights out. The three extra ones were because of the leap years …"[4]

Vladimir Vladimirovich Putin is not due to leave office until 2024, and there is no suggestion that he will alter either the way he governs or his public image in the interim. If Donald Trump runs in, and wins, the 2020 US presidential election, he too will be around until 2024. In other words, the political whirlwind that we have all endured for the past few years will continue to stretch on. Not even I, who have spent so much time revelling in Putin kitsch, can imagine the kinds of materials – digital and otherwise – that such a scenario could generate.

Note on Sources

I fell into the world of Putin kitsch quite by accident. A friend asked if I wanted to write a comparison of the Lenin and Putin leadership cults via the lens of material culture, present those findings at a conference commemorating the Russian Revolution, and possibly include my work as a chapter in the volume the conference was expected to generate. I said yes, figuring this would be a nice little side project while I worked on the book I already had under contract. I got to work in August 2015. It had to be kismet, because that was only a few months after Donald Trump formally announced that he was seeking the Republican nomination. The warm statements he made about Vladimir Putin while on the campaign trail triggered a veritable avalanche of Putin kitsch. I soon realized that I was actually working on two parallel projects – the one comparing Putin and Lenin, and another that considered the manifestations of an imagined sexual relationship between Putin and Trump. I figured that I was done with both once I had a draft of the chapter and an article in *Porn Studies* had been published. I was wrong. Somehow

N.1 Christmas ornament with Putin as all
members of the Village People.

publishers got wind of what I had been up to and got in touch. Before I knew it, I had a book contract and had crazily promised to deliver a completed manuscript within twelve months.

I have worked with material culture in some form or another for my entire academic career, so I was no stranger to building my own

archive of sources. With that said, I have never dealt with subjects –
meaning people – who were still alive. At first I did not think much
about that difference. Certainly, when it came to the items that I used
for chapters 2 and 3 of *Putin Kitsch in America*, I just dove right in
without any qualms. I still think that was the right choice, because
many examples of Putin kitsch are impermanent. That was hammered
home to me towards the end of the project when I went back to check
who had uploaded the image in figure N.1, which I had printed on
a Christmas ornament by CafePress in January 2018. I punched in
the item number (#1551495507) and found that it was gone. Well, not
quite – the picture flashed on the screen for 1–2 seconds and then
vanished. I already knew that many of the T-shirts I had purchased
in 2016 and 2017 were no longer available, but here was actual proof
that every single item in my archive could potentially disappear from
the internet. Suddenly I felt obligated to put as many illustrations as
possible into this book in order to preserve my sources for posterity.

But I did not do so blindly. After reading the pages where Ryan
Milner justified his choices about which memes to reproduce in his
book, *The World Made Meme*, I decided to apply some of the same
logic.[1] Like Milner, who talked at some length about the lasting
impact of an image on the person who had suddenly been made
famous by it, I too wanted to avoid any collateral damage. That is
why, for instance, I did not dig deeper to find the real names of
people who created the handicraft projects on Etsy.com, or who
posted images to print-on-demand services. I figured there is a
reason why some people decided to use pseudonyms and that I
needed to respect their privacy. Consequently, I only refer to information that these people provide on their listings and/or websites.

The original plan for this book also called for me to do a deep
investigation of Trump/Putin fan fiction on websites such as
Archive of Our Own, Wattpad.com, and FanFiction.net. I considered these texts to be public sources and assumed that if someone
put a story on the web, then it was no different from other kinds

of sources such as online newspaper articles. Then two things made me pause. First, I had a chat with Dr Natalie Kononenko, an outstanding folklorist, when we were both at a conference in Chicago. As I outlined my project to her, Natalie told me about one of her graduate students who was working with fan fiction, and suggested that I look into the scholarship on the ethics of researching the subject before I jumped in with both feet.

I spent the next couple of weeks doing exactly that, and I was horrified by some of what I found: writers whose real identities were discovered, causing them to be "outed" and lose their jobs. Others were ostracized from their religious communities because someone discovered that they wrote fan fiction that ran counter to the teachings of their faith.[2] Fan fiction was even dragged into one woman's rather nasty divorce. Her husband had his lawyers include a link to her writing, as well as a description of its contents, in his petition to the court. She explains his reasoning: "The argument was twofold. First, what I was writing was inappropriate as the mother of four; the fanfiction did contain several sex scenes, as did other fics I wrote. Second, I was writing it for no pay, when – according to my now-ex – I should have been job searching, which I was certainly doing at the time after losing my nearly full-time freelance client that March."[3] Thankfully, the judge overseeing the proceedings could not have cared less, and the woman eventually channelled her experiences into new, and extremely well-received, fan fiction. But hers remains a cautionary tale.

It turns out that the writers of fan fiction do expect privacy, even if their work appears in rather public settings. That is why so many use pseudonyms. And they are quite particular about which websites host their writings. Authors "expect that the shared online spaces are at least partially protected," according to Kristina Busse and Karen Hellekson, the editors of the online academic fan studies journal *Transformative Works and Cultures*. "Even though these Web sites are openly accessible, a strong internal ethos of protecting fannish spaces presents specific ethical issues for researchers."[4] For their journal, Busse and Hellekson decided that URLs to exact pages in works of fan fiction would not appear in footnotes. Instead, they opted to tread a middle ground, arguing that "negotiating expectations of privacy in the context of cultural production with academic demands of citeability is a central ethical concern for aca-fans."[5] Readers are given the blog source, user or community name, and the date of the post – in other words, enough information to track down an item, but only provided that they do a bit more work themselves.

That might work when your readers come largely from the academic world, but that may not be the case for this book, so I preferred to err on the side of extra caution. For that reason, and even though it meant I openly limited what I could do in *Putin Kitsch in America*, my analysis focused only on works available for sale on Amazon.com. I mean the main site, by the way. Kindle Worlds, the branch of the corporate giant that houses fan fiction, has not been wildly successful since its May 2013 launch. Apparently fans do not like the restrictions placed upon their works should they decide to use the site, so most have stayed away from it.[6] Moreover, there are no works that reference Vladimir Putin on Kindle Worlds anyway. People who publish Putin fiction via Amazon Digital Services LLC have zero expectations of privacy, so there is no need to agonize and worry about the potential harm I might do to their reputations by referencing the stories they have created. I leave it to others – who may have fewer ethical qualms – to discuss the Putin fan fiction that exists elsewhere. For now, I am just happy to introduce people to the wacky world of Putin kitsch.

Notes

Introduction

1 Bruno S. Sergi, *Misinterpreting Modern Russia: Western Views of Putin and His Presidency* (New York: Continuum, 2009), 149.

2 Ibid., 151.

3 John S. Earle and Klara Z. Sabirianova, "How Late to Pay? Understanding Wage Arrears in Russia," revised 2000 version of 1998 SITE Working Paper, no. 139, Stockholm, 2. https://pdfs.semanticscholar.org/ceca/3932da68428bb02261369f daadobce70fffb.pdf.

4 Ibid., 2.

5 Ibid., 173.

6 "The Russian Crisis 1998," *RaboBank Research – Economic Research*, 16 September 2013, https://economics.rabobank.com/publications/2013/september/the-russian-crisis-1998/.

7 Oleg Riabov and Tatiana Riabova, "The Remasculinization of Russia? Gender, Nationalism, and the Legitimation of Power under Vladimir Putin," *Problems of Post-Communism*, 61 (2014): 25.

8 The affair is described in Masha Gessen, *The Man without a Face: The Unlikely Rise of Vladimir Putin* (London: Granta, 2013), 121–5.

9 See Michael S. Gorham, "Putin's Language," in *Putin as Celebrity and Cultural Icon*, edited by H. Goscilo (London: Routledge, 2013), 87.

10 Steve LeVine, *Putin's Labyrinth: Spies, Murder, and the Dark Heart of the New Russia* (New York: Random House, 2008), 34.

11 Eliot Borenstein, *Overkill: Sex and Violence in Contemporary Russian Popular Culture* (Ithaca: Cornell University Press, 2008).

12 On kitsch, see "Kitsch," Merriam-Webster Dictionary, accessed 19 April 2018, https://www.merriam-webster.com/dictionary/kitsch.

13 Tomas Kulka, *Kitsch and Art* (University Park, PA: Pennsylvania State University Press, 1996), 42.

14 Catherine A. Lugg, *Kitsch: From Education to Public Policy* (New York: Falmer Press, 1999), 3.

15 Susan B. Glasser, "Putin's Cult of Personality," *The Wall Street Journal*, 16 March 2004, https://www.wsj.com/articles/SB107938501577655797.

16 Helena Goscilo, "The Ultimate Celebrity: VVP and VIP Objet d'Art," in *Celebrity and Glamour in Contemporary Russia: Shocking Chic*, edited by H. Goscilo and V. Strukov (London: Routledge, 2011), 8.

17 Ibid., 8.

18 See Nina Tumarkin, *Lenin Lives! The Lenin Cult in Soviet Russia*, enlarged ed. (Cambridge, MA: Harvard University Press, 1997), 207, 232.

19 E.A. Rees, "Leader Cults: Varieties, Preconditions and Functions," in *The Leader Cult in Communist Dictatorships: Stalin and the Eastern Bloc*, edited by B. Apor et al. (Basingstoke: Palgrave Macmillan, 2004), 21.

20 The decrees stipulated that all photographs (and negatives) of Lenin had to be turned over to the government and made it a criminal offense to reproduce, sell, or publicly exhibit portraits of Lenin without government approval. Tumarkin, *Lenin Lives!*, 237.

21 Andrei Soldatov and Irina Borogan, *The Red Web: The Struggle between Russia's Digital Dictators and the New Online Revolutionaries* (New York: PublicAffairs, 2015), 315.

22 See Catriona Kelly, "Grandpa Lenin and Uncle Stalin: Soviet Leader Cult for Little Children," in *The Leader Cult in Communist Dictatorships: Stalin and the Eastern Bloc*, edited by B. Apor et al. (Basingstoke: Palgrave Macmillan, 2004), 102–22.

23 On Thong Nhat Park, see "Thong Nhat Park," TripAdvisor, accessed 20 May 2017, https://tripadvisor.ca/ShowUserReviews-g293924-d7057006-r443945613-Thong_Nhat_Park_Lenin_Park-Hanoi.html.

24 Will Stewart, "Russia's Communists Sex-Up Lenin for Next Generation...," *Daily Mail*, 8 June 2016, http://www.dailymail.co.uk/news/article-3631747/Russia-s-Communists-sex-Lenin-generation-Revamped-revolutionary-glamorous-partner-spiced-Karl-Marx-Stalin-posters-aimed-young-voters.html.

25 Fiona Hill and Clifford G. Gaddy, *Mr. Putin: Operative in the Kremlin*, expanded ed. (Washington, DC: Brookings Institution Press, 2015), 17.

26 Elizabeth A. Wood, "Hypermasculinity as a Scenario of Power," *International Feminist Journal of Politics*, 18 (2016): 339.

27 On the ideal male physique, see Peter Weiermair, *The Hidden Image: Photographs of the Male Nude in the Nineteenth and Twentieth Centuries* (Cambridge, MA: MIT Press, 1988).

28 On Putin and "frontier masculinity," see Andrew Foxall, "Photographing Vladimir Putin: Masculinity, Nationalism and Visuality in Russian Political Culture," *Geopolitics*, 18 (2013): 141–6.

29 See Anna Arutunyan, *The Putin Mystique: Inside Russia's Power Cult* (Newbold on Stour: Skyscraper Publications, 2014), 212–15.

30 Riabov and Riabova, "Remasculinization of Russia," 26.

31 Examples can be seen in Tom Balmforth, "Russian Social-Network Guru Calls for 'Putin Shirtless Challenge,'" *Radio Free Europe Radio Liberty*, 15 August 2017, https://www.rferl.org/a/russia-putin-durov-flash-mob-bare-chested-photos/28678007.html.

32 For a discussion of the "Russian bear" as a political symbol, and how it was used to mock Dmitry Medvedev during his tenure as president of Russia, see Riabov and Riabova, "Remasculinization of Russia," 28, 30.

33 On participatory politics, see among others, Henry Jenkins, "Youth Voice, Media, and Political Engagement," in *By Any Media Necessary: The New Youth Activism*, edited by H. Jenkins et al. (New York: New York University, 2016), 1–60; and Joseph Kahne, Ellen Middaugh, and Danielle Allen, "Youth, New Media, and the Rise of Participatory Politics," in *From Voice to Influence: Understanding Citizenship in a Digital Age*, edited by Danielle Allen and Jennifer S. Light (Chicago: University of Chicago Press, 2015), 35–55.

34 See Brian McNair, *Mediated Sex: Pornography and Postmodern Culture* (London: Arnold, 1996).

Chapter One

1 Quoted in Jackson Katz, *Man Enough? Donald Trump, Hillary Clinton, and the Politics of Presidential Masculinity* (Northampton, MA: Interlink Books, 2016), xiii.

2 See Meredith Conroy, *Masculinity, Media, and the American Presidency* (Basingstoke: Palgrave Macmillan, 2015), 73–94.

3 Russell L. Peterson, *Strange Bedfellows: How Late-Night Comedy Turns Democracy into a Joke* (New Brunswick, NJ: Rutgers University Press, 2008), 19.

4   Matt Bai, *All the Truth Is Out* (New York: Vintage Books, 2014), 149.

5   Hinda Mandell, *Sex Scandals, Gender, and Power in Contemporary American Politics* (Santa Barbara, CA: Praeger, 2017), 139.

6   Peterson, *Strange Bedfellows,* 171.

7   David T.Z. Mindich, *Tuned Out: Why Americans under 40 Don't Follow the News* (New York: Oxford University Press, 2005), 52.

8   Ibid., 43.

9   Joseph N. Cappella and Kathleen Hall Jamieson, *Spiral of Cynicism: The Press and the Public Good* (New York: Oxford University Press, 1997), 29.

10 Ibid., 29.

11 David Niven, S. Robert Lichter, and Daniel Amundsen, "Our First Cartoon President: Bill Clinton and the Politics of Late Night Comedy," in *Laughing Matters: Humor and American Politics in the Media Age*, edited by J.C. Baumgartner and J.S. Morris (New York: Routledge, 2008), 153.

12 Ibid., 155. They also found that 38 per cent of the jokes referred to US president Bill Clinton.

13 Jody C. Baumgartner, "American Youth and the Effects of Online Political Humor," in *Laughing Matters: Humor and American Politics in the Media Age*, edited by J.C. Baumgartner and J.S. Morris (New York: Routledge, 2008), 132.

14 Ibid., 133.

15 Murray Edelman, *Constructing the Political Spectacle* (Chicago: University of Chicago Press, 1988), 33.

16 Dannagal Goldthwaite Young, "The Daily Show as the New Journalism: In Their Own Words," in *Laughing Matters: Humor and American Politics in the Media Age*, edited by J.C. Baumgartner and J.S. Morris (New York: Routledge, 2008), 244.

17 On participatory culture, see for example Henry Jenkins, *Textual Poachers: Television Fans and Participatory Culture* (New York: Routledge, 1992); Henry Jenkins et al., eds., *By Any Media Necessary: The New Youth Activism* (New York: New York University, 2016); and Matt Ratto and Megan Boler, eds., *DIY Citizenship: Critical Making and Social Media* (Cambridge, MA: MIT Press, 2014).

18 Lisa Colletta, "Political Satire and Postmodern Irony in the Age of Stephen Colbert and Jon Stewart," *The Journal of Popular Culture*, 42 (2009): 858.

19 Dannagal Goldthwaite Young and Sarah E. Ersalew, "Jon Stewart a Heretic? Surely You Jest: Political Participation and Discussion among Viewers of Late-Night Comedy Programming," in *The Stewart/Colbert Effect: Essays on*

the Real Impacts of Fake News, edited by A. Amarasingam (Jefferson, NC: McFarland and Company, 2011), 102.

20 Lynn Hunt, "Pornography and the French Revolution," in *The Invention of Pornography: Obscenity and the Origins of Modernity, 1500–1800*, edited by Lynn Hunt (New York: Zone Books, 1993), 306.

21 See Orlando Figes and Boris Kolonitskii, *Interpreting the Russian Revolution: The Language and Symbols of 1917* (New Haven: Yale University Press, 1999), 11–14.

22 Mandell, *Sex Scandals*, 22.

23 Ibid.

24 Brian McNair, *Fake News: Falsehood, Fabrication and Fantasy in Journalism* (London: Routledge, 2018), ix.

25 Dan Gillmor, *We the Media: Grassroots Journalism By the People, For the People* (Sebastopol, CA: O'Reilly Media, 2004), 92.

26 On MoveOn.org, see "Move On," Wikipedia, accessed 10 May 2018, https://en.wikipedia.org/wiki/MoveOn.org. For the contest, see Gillmor, *We the Media*, 100.

27 Gillmor, *We the Media*, 177.

28 Joe Trippi, *The Revolution Will Not Be Televised*, rev. ed. (New York: Harper, 2008), 145–6.

29 Ibid., xx–xxi.

30 Taylor Owen, *Disruptive Power: The Crisis of the State in the Digital Age* (New York: Oxford University Press, 2015), 113.

31 Ibid., 194.

32 Robert D. Dean, "Masculinity as Ideology: John F. Kennedy and the Domestic Politics of Foreign Policy," *Diplomatic History*, 22 (1998): 33.

33 Ibid., 46.

34 Jackson Katz refers to the leaders as "embodied proxies." See Katz, *Man Enough?*, 70.

35 Quoted in Conroy, *Masculinity*, 73–4.

Chapter Two

1 Sarah Begley, "Is the Adult Coloring Book Trend Coming to an End?," *Time.com*, 3 March 2017, http://time.com/4689069/coloring-book-bubble-bursts/.

2 Kate Harrison, "The Adult Coloring Craze Continues and There Is No End in Sight," *Forbes*, 2 February 2016, https://www.forbes.com/sites/kateharrison/2016/02/02the-adult-coloring-craze-continues-and-there-is-no-end-in-sight/.

3   It must be noted that the quality of Kirkwood's English in her description matches the quality of the book overall. Some of the illustrations are incomplete or are so faint that it is hard to make them out.

4   Melia Robinson, "This Woman Is Making a Fortune Selling Coloring Books for Adults," *Business Insider*, 8 December 2015, http://www.businessinsider.com/jenean-morrison-adult-coloring-books-2015-12.

5   http://www.bowker.com/news/2017/Self-Publishing-ISBNs-Climbed-8-Between-2015-2016.html, accessed 19 December 2017.

6   https://www.kickstarter.com/projects/adventurebuddies/adventure-buddies-adult-coloring-book, accessed 19 January 2017.

7   See https://www.thecolor.com/Coloring/Vladimir-Putin.aspx and http://17co.cf/vladimir-putin-coloring-pages.html, both accessed 6 November 2017.

8   In 2008, Putin's approval rating was at 87 per cent. See Fiona Hill and Clifford G. Gaddy, *Mr. Putin: Operative in the Kremlin*, expanded ed. (Washington, DC: Brookings Institution Press, 2015), 245.

9   This is one of the main points made by Hill and Gaddy in *Mr. Putin*.

10 Alessandra Antola, "Photographing Mussolini," in *The Cult of the Duce: Mussolini and the Italians*, edited by Stephen Gundle, Christopher Duggan, and Giuliana Pieri (Manchester: Manchester University Press, 2013), 187.

11 Nia-Malika Henderson and Carrie Budoff Brown, "Paparazzo Snaps Shirtless Obama," *Politico.com*, 22 December 2008. https://www.politico.com/story/2008/12/paparazzo-snaps-shirtless-obama-016802.

12 Mark Frazier, *Ron Paul Revolution: History in the Making* (Jackson, MI: Mark Proffit, 2008), 20.

13 Figure given on the CafePress Wikipedia page; see "Cafepress," *Wikipedia*, accessed 15 January 2018, https://en.wikipedia.org/wiki/CafePress.

14 The footage can be seen at https://www.youtube.com/watch?v=iGSJCDw-3ZBw, accessed 23 January 2018.

15 Ryan M. Milner, *The World Made Meme: Public Conversations and Participatory Media* (Cambridge, MA: MIT Press, 2016), 212.

16 Hill and Gaddy, *Mr. Putin*, 221.

17 Janis L. Edwards, "Drawing Politics in Pink and Blue," *PS: Political Science and Politics*, 40 (2007): 249.

18 Zazzle was founded in 2005, with some funding from Google investors John Doerr and Ram Shriram. It is headquartered in Redwood City, California. The company says that it has over 300 million unique items for sale on its website. See "Zazzle," *Wikipedia*, accessed 15 January 2018, https://en.wikipedia.org/wiki/Zazzle.

19 The image can be seen at https://fineartamerica.com/featured/super-powers-dan-youra.html, accessed 28 January 2018.

20 Joan L. Conners, "Barack versus Hillary: Race, Gender, and Political Cartoon Imagery of the 2008 Presidential Primaries," *American Behavioral Scientist*, 54 (2010): 304.

21 See definitions for "Spanked," Urban Dictionary, accessed 28 January 2018, https://www.urbandictionary.com/define.php?term=spanked.

22 Charlotte Brunel, *The T-shirt Book* (New York: Assouline, 2002), 12.

23 Major American retailers such as Hanes or Sears sold plain white T-shirts for roughly 24 cents a piece. See Alice Harris, *The White T* (New York: Harper Collins, 1996), 20.

24 Brunel, *The T-shirt Book*, 120.

25 Harris, *The White T*, 122.

26 It is worth noting that the same website sells women's bathing suits that feature close-up pictures of Hillary Clinton and Donald Trump as well as men's swim trunks with pictures of Trump and North Korean leader Kim Jong Un on them.

27 Beloved Shirts is headquartered in Provo, Utah. Company founder Jeremiah Robinson appeared on the American television program *Shark Tank* in episode 727 (March 2016), but his pitch did not result in a deal with the program's wealthy investors. The firm sells its print-on-demand textiles through Amazon.com and its own website. The Putin design is available on hoodies, T-shirts, and a men's tank top, as well as the bathing suit shown here.

28 Julie A. Cassiday and Emily D. Johnson, "A Personality Cult for the Postmodern Age: Reading Vladimir Putin's Public Persona," in *Putin as Celebrity and Cultural Icon*, edited by H. Goscilo (London: Routledge, 2013), 53.

29 Thomas Smale, "Is Amazon's 'Merch' the Next Big Thing?," *Entrepreneur. com*, 31 May 2017, https://www.entrepreneur.com/article/295010.

30 Catherine Clifford, "How Two Guys in Their 20s Built a $150,000 Side Hustle Selling T-shirts on Amazon," CNBC, 12 October 2016, https://www.cnbc.com/2016/10/12/how-two-guys-in-their-20s-built-a-150000-side-hustle-selling-T-shirts-on-amazon.html.

31 Helena Goscilo, "The Ultimate Celebrity: VVP and VIP Objet d'art," in *Celebrity and Glamour in Contemporary Russia: Shocking Chic*, edited by H. Goscilo and V. Strukov (London: Routledge, 2011), 37.

32 Jane Caputi, "From (Castrating) Bitch to (Big) Nuts: Genital Politics in 2016 Election Campaign Paraphernalia," in *Nasty Women and Bad Hombres:*

Gender and Race in the 2016 US Presidential Election, edited by Christine Kray, Tamar Carroll, and Hinda Mandell (Rochester: University of Rochester Press, 2018), 25–41.

33 Ruth Reader, "A Brief History of Etsy, from 2005 Brooklyn Launch to 2015 IPO," *Venturebeat.com*, 5 March 2015, https://venturebeat.com/2015/03/05/a-brief-history-of-etsy-from-2005-brooklyn-launch-to-2015-ipo/.

34 Ibid.

35 Taylor Majewski, "A Brief History of Etsy on Its 10th Anniversary," *Built-innyc.com*, 5 November 2015, https://www.builtinnyc.com/2015/11/04/brief-history-etsy.

36 https://www.etsy.com/au/listing/266093127/vladimir-putin-politically-incorrect, accessed 20 December 2017.

37 The pattern is mentioned in Goscilo, "Russia's Ultimate Celebrity," 8.

38 See, for instance, the articles in Amarnath Amarasingam, ed., *The Stewart/Colbert Effect: Essays on the Real Impacts of Fake News* (Jefferson, NC: McFarland and Company, 2011).

39 Lisa Colletta, "Political Satire and Postmodern Irony in the Age of Stephen Colbert and Jon Stewart," *The Journal of Popular Culture*, 42 (2009): 859.

40 Ibid., 868.

41 The same can be said for the sources analyzed by the contributors to *Crafting Dissent: Handicraft as Protest from the American Revolution to the Pussyhats*, an anthology of articles edited by Hinda Mandell (under contract with Rowman and Littlefield).

Chapter Three

1 See the articles contained in Lynn Hunt, ed., *The Invention of Pornography*; and see Orlando Figes and Boris Kolonitskii, *Interpreting the Russian Revolution*. An article by Lisa Z. Sigel also considers homemade pornography – some of it with political overtones – that was created in the United States between the 1830s and the 1930s. See Lisa Z. Sigel, "Handmade and Homemade: Vernacular Expressions of American Sexual History," *Journal of the History of Sexuality*, 25 (2016): 437–62.

2 Laura Kipnis, *Bound and Gagged: Pornography and the Politics of Fantasy in America* (Durham: Duke University Press, 1999), 123.

3 See Adrienne Raphel, "Why Adults Are Buying Coloring Books (For Themselves)," *The New Yorker*, 12 July 2015, https://www.newyorker.com/business/currency/why-adults-are-buying-coloring-books-for-themselves;

Mark Potts, "Growing Up Is Hard to Do," *Campaign*, 10 February 2016, https://www.campaignlive.com/article/growing-hard/1382855; and Gabrielle George, "Trend Breakdown: The Peter Pan Market," *Dconstruct*, 2017, http://dconstruct.doner.com/trend-breakdown-the-peter-pan-market/.

4   Geoffrey Baym, "Serious Comedy: Expanding the Boundaries of Political Discourse," in *Laughing Matters: Humor and American Politics in the Media Age*, edited by J.C. Baumgartner and J.S. Morris (New York: Routledge, 2008), 29.

5   Chris Lamb, *Drawn to Extremes: The Use and Abuse of Editorial Cartoons* (New York: Columbia University Press, 2004), 39–40.

6   Karrin V. Anderson and Kristina H. Sheeler, *Governing Codes: Gender, Metaphor, and Political Identity* (Lantham: Lexington Books, 2005), 20.

7   Kristen V. Brown, "Inside the Wild, Weird World of Donald Trump Parody Porn and Sex Toys," *Splinter*, 19 September 2016, https://splinternews.com/inside-the-wild-weird-world-of-donald-trump-parody-por-1793861997.

8   See https://www.youtube.com/watch?v=Ve6I92hEozo.

9   See "CatDog," *Wikipedia*, accessed 18 January 2017, https://en.wikipedia.org/wiki/CatDog.

10   Brian McNair, *Porno? Chic! How Pornography Changed the World and Made It a Better Place* (London: Routledge, 2013), 30.

11   Karrin Anderson, "'Rhymes with Blunt': Pornification and U.S. Political Culture," *Rhetoric and Public Affairs*, 14 (2011): 335.

12   Valerie Sperling, *Sex, Politics, and Putin: Political Legitimacy in Russia* (Oxford: Oxford University Press, 2015), 16–17.

13   Both items described in this paragraph can be seen in Alison Rowley, "'Trump and Putin Sittin' in a Tree': Material Culture, Slash and the Pornographication of the 2016 US Presidential Election," *Porn Studies*, 4 (2017): 384, 385.

14   See "Socialist Fraternal Kiss," *Wikipedia*, accessed 3 January 2018, https://en.wikipedia.org/wiki/Socialist_fraternal_kiss.

15   The painting can be seen at "My God, Help Me to Survive This Deadly Love," *Wikipedia*, accessed 3 January 2018, https://en.wikipedia.org/wiki/My_God,_Help_Me_to_Survive_This_Deadly_Love.

16   Marcel Danesi, *The History of the Kiss!* (New York: Palgrave Macmillan, 2013), 3.

17   https://www.theguardian.com/world/2016/aug/12/vandals-censor-image-of-putin-snogging-trump-lithuania, accessed 21 November 2016.

18   Carmine Sarrachino and Kevin M. Scott, *The Porning of America* (Boston: Beacon Press, 2008), 158.

19 An updated version of this image, found on Etsy in January and with a different seller listed, changed the colour of the woman's hair and named her as Stormy Daniels in its caption.

20 Hinda Mandell, *Sex Scandals, Gender, and Power in Contemporary American Politics* (Santa Barbara, CA: Praeger, 2017), 41.

21 Mark Hay, "The Oral History of the Money Shot," *Vice.com*, 12 December 2016, https://www.vice.com/en_us/article/qkbwd5/an-oral-history-of-the-moneyshot.

22 See "Creampie," Urban Dictionary, accessed 6 January 2018, https://www.urbandictionary.com/define.php?term=Creampie.

23 See Molly Redden, "Donald Trump Paid Porn Star $130,000 to Stay Silent over Alleged Affair – Report," *The Guardian*, 13 January 2018, https://www.theguardian.com/us-news/2018/jan/12/trump-affair-adult-film-star-stormy-daniels; and Ben Jacobs, "Porn Star Alana Evans Says She Was Invited to Trump's Hotel Room in 2006," *The Guardian*, 14 January 2018, https://www.theguardian.com/us-news/2018/jan/13/trump-porn-star-alana-evans-stormy-daniels-report.

24 Howard Blum, "How Ex-Spy Christopher Steele Compiled His Explosive Trump-Russia Dossier," *Vanity Fair.com*, 30 March 2017, https://www.vanityfair.com/news/2017/03/how-the-explosive-russian-dossier-was-compiled-christopher-steele.

25 See Michael Isikoff and David Corn, *Russian Roulette: The Inside Story of Putin's War on America and the Election of Donald Trump* (New York: Twelve, 2018), 148–50.

26 T.A. Frank, "The Alleged Trump-Putin 'Golden Shower' Fiasco, Explained," *Vanity Fair.com*, 11 January 2017, https://www.vanityfair.com/news/2017/01/trump-russia-report-explained.

27 Margot D. Weiss, "Mainstreaming Kink: The Politics of BDSM Representation in U.S. Popular Media," *Journal of Homosexuality*, 50 (2006): 124.

Chapter Four

1 According to the Pew Research Center, in March 2000, only 1 per cent of US adults had home broadband service, although 52 per cent of Americans used the internet. By November 2016, 75 per cent of Americans had broadband at home (12 per cent of those who did not used smartphones to access the internet), and an estimated 89 per cent of US adults presently use the internet. The percentages are highest in the youngest age groups: in 2018, 98 per cent

of eighteen-to-twenty-nine-year-olds use the internet, as do 97 per cent of the thirty-to-forty-nine-year-old cohort. See http://www.pewinternet.org/fact-sheet/internet-broadband/, accessed 20 February 2018.

2 Rebecca W. Black, *Adolescents and Online Fan Fiction* (New York: Peter Lang, 2008), xiii.

3 Kristina Busse, "My Life Is a wip on My lj: Slashing the Slasher and the Reality of Celebrity and Internet Performances," in *Fan Fiction and Fan Communities in the Age of the Internet*, edited by Karen Hellekson and Kristina Busse (Jefferson, nc: McFarland and Co., 2006), 215.

4 See *Emma and the Vampires*; *The Vampire of Northanger*; and *Pride and Prejudice and Zombies*. All three titles are available at Amazon.com.

5 Review by Richard Nagl, posted to Amazon.com on 25 January 2014. On the challenges of trusting Amazon reviews, see Whitney Phillips and Ryan M. Milner, *The Ambivalent Internet: Mischief, Oddity, and Antagonism Online* (Cambridge: Polity, 2017), 3, 50.

6 www.jeffpollard.webs.com, accessed 4 June 2018.

7 Review by rfortney, posted to Amazon.com on 14 November 2012.

8 In reality, the gymnast linked to Putin was Alina Kabaeva, who won two Olympic gold medals in rhythmic gymnastics before retiring. From 2007 to 2014, Kabaeva served as a State Duma deputy for Putin's United Russia party. She was also rumoured to have had one or two children with Putin, who has never commented on their relationship. See Harriet Alexander, "Vladimir Putin Marriage Break-Up: Was the Gymnast to Blame?," *The Telegraph*, 6 June 2013, https://www.telegraph.co.uk/news/worldnews/vladimir-putin/10104682/Vladimir-Putin-marriage-break-up-was-the-Russian-gymnast-to-blame.html.

9 These arguments are described in Engin Isin and Evelyn Ruppert, "Citizen Snowden," *International Journal of Communication*, 11 (2017): 843–57.

10 Ibid., 854.

11 See John Breech, "Patriots' Robert Kraft: Vladimir Putin Stole My Super Bowl Ring," *CBSSports.com*, 15 June 2013, https://www.cbssports.com/nfl/news/patriots-robert-kraft-vladimir-putin-stole-my-super-bowl-ring/.

12 For information about the expression, see "Putin Khuylo!," *Wikipedia*, accessed 7 June 2018, https://en.wikipedia.org/wiki/Putin_khuylo!

13 Shaun Walker, "Ukraine Minister's Abusive Remarks about Putin Spark Diplomatic Row," *The Guardian*, 15 June 2014, https://www.theguardian.com/world/2014/jun/15/ukraine-minister-deshchytsia-abusive-putin-russia.

14 For examples, see Svetlana Fokina, "The Etymology of the Word: 'Huylo' (as in 'Putin Huylo')," *Voices of Ukraine*, 6 May 2014, https://maidantranslations.com/2014/05/10/the-etymology-of-the-word-huylo-as-in-putin-huylo/comment-page-1/.

15 Meredith Conroy, *Masculinity, Media, and the American Presidency* (Basingstoke: Palgrave Macmillan, 2015), 73.

16 In 2008 Putin's government recognized the Republic of Abkhazia as an independent state, but Georgia, and most members of the United Nations, consider it to be under Russian occupation. The situation is similar for the Republic of South Ossetia.

17 Michael Crowley and Julia Ioffe, "Why Putin Hates Hillary," *Politico.com*, 25 July 2016, https://www.politico.com/story/2016/07/clinton-putin-226153.

18 Charlotte Templin, "Hillary Clinton as Threat to Gender Norms: Cartoon Images of the First Lady," *Journal of Communication Inquiry*, 23 (1999): 25–6.

19 Ibid., 32.

20 Karrin Anderson, "'Rhymes with Blunt': Pornification and U.S. Political Culture," 343.

21 The fake biography provided for the author says, "Raised in a laboratory setting, Trashcan Jones is a Malaysian orangutan who was taught to type at a young age. She enjoys masturbation, fresh fruit and grooming her fellow apes." Amazon sells two other titles by the same author – one about teenagers getting revenge on their high school bully and the other describing a one-night stand between Beyoncé and a cowboy.

22 See John King, "Clinton, Putin Exchange Complaints in Oslo Meeting," *CNN.com*, 2 November 1999, http://edition.cnn.com/WORLD/europe/9911/02/clinton.putin/.

23 Margot D. Weiss, "Mainstreaming Kink: The Politics of BDSM Representation in U.S. Popular Media," *Journal of Homosexuality*, 50 (2006): 114.

Chapter Five

1 On the early history of slash, see Francesca Coppa, "A Brief History of Media Fandom," in *Fan Fiction and Fan Communities in the Age of the Internet*, edited by Karen Hellekson and Kristina Busse (Jefferson, NC: McFarland and Co., 2006), 41–59.

2 Henry Jenkins, *Fans, Bloggers, and Gamers: Exploring Participatory Culture* (New York: New York University Press, 2006), 142.

3 Kristina Busse, "My Life as a WIP on My LJ," 214.

4   Alison Flood, "Donald Trump Triumphs as Hero of 'Sensual and Tawdry' Erotic Novel," *The Guardian*, 26 January 2016, https://www.theguardian.com/books/2016/jan/26/donald-trump-erotic-novel-temptation-billionaire-bellboy-elijah-daniel-amazon.

5   On the spectrum of fetishes found in these works, see Alison Rowley, "'Trump and Putin Sittin' in a Tree.'"

6   See Jackson Katz, *Man Enough?*, 77.

7   Valerie Sperling, *Sex, Politics, and Putin*, 17.

8   Ibid., 30.

9   Ibid., 104.

10 See, for instance, Tatiana Mikhailova, "Putin as the Father of the Nation: His Family and Other Animals," in *Putin as Celebrity and Cultural Icon*, edited by H. Goscilo (London: Routledge, 2013), 71.

11 Ibid., 75.

12 Russian-American journalist Masha Gessen, for example, debunks several of Putin's most well-known escapades in her biography of Putin. See Gessen, *The Man without a Face*, 297.

13 Klaus Dodds, "Graduated and Paternal Sovereignty: Stephen Harper, Operation Nanook 10, and the Canadian Arctic," *Environment and Planning D: Society and Space*, 30 (2012): 1000.

14 Steven Blum makes this point in his article on Trump/Putin slash. See Blum, "Inside the World of Erotic Trump Fan Fiction," *Mel Magazine*, 25 January 2018, https://melmagazine.com/inside-the-world-of-erotic-trump-fan-fiction-23b812a9914e.

15 See, for example, German Lopez, "Your Trump-Putin Slashfic Isn't Funny. It's Homophobic," *Vox.com*, 11 July 2017, https://www.vox.com/identities/2017/7/11/15948206/trump-putin-liberal-homophobia.

16 *Casino in the Kremlin* reverses the binary found in the other stories since the author says Putin has "a penis commensurate with the dictator's relative stature." The size of Trump's genitals is not mentioned, but readers are told that the American's pubic hair has a comb-over.

17 Catherine M. Roach, *Happily Ever After: The Romance Story in Popular Culture* (Bloomington: Indiana University Press, 2016), 96.

18 Katz, *Man Enough?*, x.

19 Kristen V. Brown, "Inside the Wild, Weird World of Donald Trump Parody Porn and Sex Toys."

20 On Russia's treatment of the LGBTQ community, see Dan Healey, *Russian Homophobia from Stalin to Sochi* (London: Bloomsbury Academic, 2018).

21 Cynthia K. Drenovsky, "Game Changer: The Clinton Scandal and American Sexuality," in *Sex Scandals in American Politics*, edited by Alison Dagnes (New York: Continuum International Publishing Group, 2011), 17.

22 See Frank Bruni, "The 2000 Campaign: The Texas Governor; Bush Calls on Gore to Denounce Clinton Affair," *The New York Times*, 12 August 2000, https://www.nytimes.com/2000/08/12/us/2000-campaign-texas-governor-bush-calls-gore-denounce-clinton-affair.html.

23 See https://www.mail-archive.com/ctrl@listserv.aol.com/msg60359.html, accessed 21 June 2018.

24 See Niven, Lichter, and Amundsen, "Our First Cartoon President: Bill Clinton and the Politics of Late Night Comedy," 152.

25 On the expression, see https://www.phrases.org.uk/meanings/close-your-eyes-and-think-of-england.html, accessed 20 June 2018.

26 On transvestite porn and sissification, see Kipnis, *Bound and Gagged*, 66–78; and "Feminization," *Wikipedia*, accessed 20 June 2018, https://en.wikipedia.org/wiki/Feminization_(activity). On Amazon.com, Sparks is listed as the author of dozens of stories about sissification as well as some transgender erotica. None of the other titles appears to be political in nature, however.

27 Dan F. Hahn, *Political Communication: Rhetoric, Government, and Citizens* (State College, PA: Strata Publishing, 1998), 134.

28 Katz, *Man Enough?*, ix.

29 See Kristina Busse and Karen Hellekson, "Introduction: Work in Progress," in *Fan Fiction and Fan Communities in the Age of the Internet*, edited by Karen Hellekson and Kristina Busse (Jefferson, NC: McFarland and Co., 2006), 11.

30 See http://www.whitehousemuseum.org/floor2/lincoln-bedroom.htm, accessed 21 June 2018.

31 David Chidester, "'A Big Wind Blew Up during the Night': America as Sacred Space in South Africa," in *American Sacred Space*, edited by David Chidester and Edward T. Linenthal (Bloomington: Indiana University Press, 1995), 290.

32 Ibid., 294.

33 Kipnis, *Bound and Gagged*, 132.

34 Ibid.

35 Review posted on Amazon.com on 8 December 2017.

Chapter Six

1 See Jeff Taylor, "'21st Century Bastards,' the Fake Action Figures We Wish Were Real," *LGBTQ Nation*, 6 March 2017, https://www.lgbtqnation. com/2017/03/21st-century-bastards-fake-action-figures-wish-real/. The article contains quotations from Chris Barker and shows the prototypes.

2 Michele Zappavigna, *Discourse of Twitter and Social Media* (London: Continuum, 2012), 50.

3 For those who may not know precisely what the term means, a troll is someone who deliberately sows conflict by posting provocative and/or off-topic messages to social media sites.

4 Whitney Phillips and Ryan M. Milner, *The Ambivalent Internet*, 78–9.

5 On YouTube, see Jean Burgess and Joshua Green, *YouTube: Online Video and Participatory Culture* (Cambridge: Polity Press, 2009).

6 "The YouTube-ification of Politics: Candidates Losing Control," *CNN.com*, 18 July 2007, http://www.cnn.com/2007/POLITICS/07/18/youtube.effect/ index.html.

7 These incidents are discussed in Vassia Gueorguieva, "Voters, MySpace, and YouTube: The Impact of Alternative Communication Channels on the 2006 Election Cycle and Beyond," *Social Science Computer Review*, 26 (2008): 288–300.

8 Trippi, *The Revolution Will Not Be Televised*, 264–5.

9 W. Lance Bennett, Dean Freelon, and Chris Wells, "Changing Citizen Identity and the Rise of a Participatory Media Culture," in *Handbook of Research on Civic Engagement in Youth*, edited by L.R. Sherrod, J. Torney-Purta, and C.A. Flanagan (Hoboken, NJ: John Wiley and Sons, 2010), 403.

10 See, for example, Katy Pearce and Adnan Hajizada, "No Laughing Matter: Humor as a Means of Dissent in the Digital Era: The Case of Authoritarian Azerbaijan," *Demokratizatsiya*, 22 (2014): 67–85.

11 Zappavigna, *Discourse of Twitter*, 117–20.

12 *Best Putin Memes: Funniest Memes* (CreateSpace, 2016).

13 Morgan Evans, "The Answers for the Worst Visual Puns of All Time," *Huffington Post*, 9 May 2010, https://www.huffingtonpost.ca/entry/the-answers-for-the-worst_n_490720.

14 See "Putin on the Ritz," *Wikipedia*, accessed 22 July 2018, https://en.wikipedia. org/wiki/Puttin%27_On_the_Ritz.

15 https://www.youtube.com/watch?v=fnVwjw2Un4k, accessed 22 July 2018.

16 Daria Gonzales, "Putin ... on the Ritz," *Russia Beyond*, 13 March 2012, https://www.rbth.com/articles/2012/03/13/putin_on_the_ritz_15050.html.

17 See https://bigtengirl.wordpress.com/2012/04/08/putin-on-the-ritz/, accessed 22 July 2018.

18 See https://www.youtube.com/watch?v=7emG7bMqJiU, accessed 6 August 2018.

19 See https://www.youtube.com/watch?v=dReOdQmt-Qk, accessed 22 July 2018.

20 See, for instance, Dawn Ennis, "Putin and the Ritz: This Hilarious Randy Rainbow Video Will Make Your Day," LGBTQ *Nation*, 7 March 2017, https://www.lgbtqnation.com/2017/03/putin-ritz-hilarious-randy-rainbow-video-will-make-day/.

21 "Russia's (Non) War on Memes?," BBC *Trending*, 16 April 2015, https://www.bbc.com/news/blogs-trending-32302645.

22 For information on the game, see Eric Shorey, "'Putin Gay Dress-Up' Video Game Gives Vladimir a Fab Fashion Makeover," Newnownext.com, 5 March 2014, http://www.newnownext.com/give-putin-a-gay-makeover-with-this-video-game/03/2014/. The number of users is given in "LGBT Rights in Russia," *Wikipedia*, accessed 7 August 2018, https://en.wikipedia.org/wiki/LGBT_rights_in_Russia.

23 Shorey, "'Putin Gay Dress-Up' Video Game Gives Vladimir a Fab Fashion Makeover."

24 Amanda Lenhart et al., "Teens, Video Games, and Civics," *Pew Research Center*, 16 September 2008, http://www.pewinternet.org/2008/09/16/teens-video-games-and-civics/.

25 Those who suggest that gaming is influential often refer to games such as the Sims to make their case. For a discussion of the subject after the initial Pew report, see Helen Haste, "Citizenship Education: A Critical Look at a Contested Field," in *Handbook of Research on Civic Engagement in Youth*, edited by L.R. Sherrod, J. Torney-Purta, and C.A. Flanagan (Hoboken, NJ: John Wiley and Sons, 2010), 161–88.

26 These figures are all given in Barbara Flueckiger, "The iPhone Apps: A Digital Culture of Interactivity," in *Moving Data: The iPhone and the Future of Media*, edited by Pelle Snickars and Patrick Vonderau (New York: Columbia University Press, 2012), 172–3.

27 Mia Consalvo, "Slingshot to Victory: Games, Play, and the iPhone," in *Moving Data: The iPhone and the Future of Media*, edited by Pelle Snickars and Patrick Vonderau (New York: Columbia University Press, 2012), 184, 186.

28 Michael Murphy, David J. Phillips, and Karen Pollock, "Doing It in the Cloud: Google, Apple, and the Shaping of DIY Culture," in *DIY Citizenship: Critical Making and Social Media*, edited by Matt Ratto and Megan Boler (Cambridge, MA: MIT Press, 2014), 250.

29 Ibid., 253.

30 Howard Gardner and Katie Davis, *The App Generation* (New Haven: Yale University Press, 2013), 142.

31 The game was apparently never finished. See "Vladimir Putin Is a Zombie Slayer in an Upcoming Video Game for Mobile Devices," *Business Insider*, 1 October 2013, https://www.businessinsider.com.au/vladimir-putin-is-battling-zombies-in-an-upcoming-video-game-2013-10.

32 Matthew Humphries, "180 New Games Launch on Steam Every Week," *PCMag.com*, 29 June 2018, https://www.pcmag.com/news/362177/180-new-games-launch-on-steam-every-week.

33 The figures are from the Wikipedia page devoted to Steam. See "Steam," *Wikipedia*, accessed 7 August 2018, https://en.wikipedia.org/wiki/Steam_(software).

34 Patrick Klepek, "How Valve's Hands-Off Approach Allowed the Homophobic 'Gay World' on Steam," *Vice.com*, 24 January 2018, https://waypoint.vice.com/en_us/article/7xeyvg/how-valves-hands-off-approach-allowed-the-homophobic-gay-world-on-steam.

35 See http://crappy-games.wikia.com/wiki/Nikita_%22Ghost_RUS%22_Games, accessed 15 July 2018.

36 For a discussion of Porn 2.0, see David Slayden, "Debbie Does Dallas Again and Again: Pornography, Technology, and Market Innovation," in *Porn.com: Making Sense of Online Pornography*, edited by Feona Attwood (New York: Peter Lang, 2010), 54–68.

37 Ibid., 66.

38 Alexa Internet measures and ranks the web traffic of more than 30 million websites. Dennis D. Waskul and Cheryl L. Radeloff, "'How Do I Rate? Web Sites and Gendered Erotic Looking Glasses," in *Porn.com: Making Sense of Online Pornography*, edited by Feona Attwood (New York: Peter Lang, 2010), 202.

39 On Pornhub, see "Pornhub," *Wikipedia*, accessed 15 July 2018. https://en.wikipedia.org/wiki/Pornhub.

40 See "Russia's Five Most Memorable Censorship Moments of 2016," *Mapping Global Media Policy*, 30 December 2016, http://www.globalmediapolicy.net/node/16183; and Damien Sharkov, "How Vladimir Putin Has Cracked Down on Russia's Internet," *Newsweek*, 31 July 2017, https://www.newsweek.com/how-vladimir-putin-cracked-down-russias-internet-644176.

41 Dave Lee, "Deepfakes Porn Has Serious Consequences," *bbc.com*, 3 February 2018, https://www.bbc.com/news/technology-42912529; and Megan Farokhmanesh, "Deepfakes Are Disappearing from Parts of the Web, But They're Not Going Away," *The Verge*, 9 February 2018, https://www.theverge.com/2018/2/9/16986602/deepfakes-banned-reddit-ai-faceswap-porn.

42 Christopher Hooton, "Pornhub Begs Users to Stop Uploading Video Clips of Brazil Getting Beaten 7–1," *Independent*, 9 July 2014, https://www.independent.co.uk/sport/football/international/pornhub-pleads-users-to-stop-uploading-videos-of-brazil-getting-fked-by-germany-in-the-world-cup-9594287.html.

43 Henry Jenkins, "Youth Voice, Media, and Political Engagement," 2.

Conclusion

1 "The Story Behind TIME's Trump and Putin 'Summit Crisis' Cover," *Time.com*, 19 July 2018, http://time.com/5342562/donald-trump-vladimir-putin-summit-crisis-cover/.

2 David Moye, "Wall Street Bull Covered in Sex Toys, Ridden by 'Vladimir Putin,'" *HuffPost*, 17 July 2018. https://www.huffingtonpost.ca/entry/bull-vladimir-putin-sex-toys_us_5b4e717ee4b0de86f487d3b8.

3 Lydia O'Connor, "New York Times Called Out for Homophobic Trump-Putin Cartoon," *HuffPost*, 16 July 2018, https://www.huffingtonpost.ca/entry/new-york-times-homophobic-trump-putin-cartoon_us_5b4cd4c8e4b0e7c958fe2229.

4 Alexander Solzhenitsyn, *One Day in the Life of Ivan Denisovich*, trans. M. Hayward and R. Hingley (New York: Bantam Books, 1963), 203.

Note on Sources

1 Milner, *The World Made Meme*. Milner also addressed some of these methodological issues in the more recent book that he co-authored with Whitney Phillips, *The Ambivalent Internet*.

2 Jolie Fontenot, "Twilight's True Believers," in *Fic: Why Fanfiction Is Taking Over the World*, edited by Anne Jamison (Dallas, TX: Smart Pop, 2013), 191.

3 Cyndy Aleo, "On Writing – and Being – a Mary Sue," in *Fic: Why Fanfiction Is Taking Over the World*, edited by Anne Jamison (Dallas, TX: Smart Pop, 2013), 210.

4   Kristina Busse and Karen Hellekson, "Identity, Ethics, and Fan Privacy," in *Fan Culture: Theory/Practice*, edited by K. Larsen and L. Zubernis, (Newcastle upon Tyne: Cambridge Scholars Publishing, 2012), 42.

5   Acafans are academics who happen to also be fans. Ibid., 42.

6   Jeff Roberts, "Amazon's Fan-Fiction Portal Kindle Worlds Is a Bust for Fans, and for Writers Too," Gigaom.com, 17 August 2014, https://gigaom.com/2014/08/17/amazons-fan-fiction-portal-kindle-worlds-is-a-bust-for-fans-and-for-writers-too/.

Index